Traveling the Way

Traveling

By Drusilla McGowen
Pictures by A. Daniel Zook

the WAY

Rod and Staff Publishers, Inc.
P.O. Box 3, Hwy. 172
Crockett, Kentucky 41413
Telephone: 606-522-4348

Published in 1977 by Rod and Staff Publishers, Inc.
by special arrangement with The Seabury Press.

Printed in U.S.A.

ISBN 978-07399-0129-8

Catalog no. 2445

10 11 12 13 — 22 21 20 19 18 17 16

Contents

Foreword

Cleon is a Gentile slave boy who is introduced to Judaism and Christianity. The story is built around the time of the early persecution of the Christians. It illustrates well what Jesus said: "I came not to send peace, but a sword."

The story acquaints readers with the problems of the Christians and with a cultural setting different from our own.

We have chosen to reprint this book because the message it contains is profitable for all who will read it.

The Publishers

1

Cleon's pen scratched over a large sheet of papyrus. He worked slowly and carefully as he copied each letter. His tired eyes moved from the manuscript before him to the sheet on which he was working.

It was hot. Cleon's fingers were sticky. He hated Jerusalem. He hated working all alone in the library. He hated being a slave. Most of all, he hated his master, Marcus Vitruvius. Vitruvius was a Roman agent with the rank of quaestor, or treasurer. He was constantly on the move; no sooner were they settled in one place than an order would come to move to another. Then Vitruvius would be in an even worse humor than usual; and, at best, he was not a kindly man.

Sounds of laughter and shouting came to Cleon from the street below. Every day just before noon, a group of boys played games in the courtyard of the next building. Cleon threw down his pen and ran to the window. He had never done this before, but today he could not resist. If his master ever caught him, he would be punished. Cleon watched the boys. They seemed to be about his own age, twelve, and they were having fun.

Close to tears, Cleon walked back to his work. He blinked. "Only babies cry," he told himself.

Not once had Cleon played a game with other boys. He had never had a friend his own age. Alexander, a slave shopkeeper, was a good friend; but he was old. Cleon listened to the shouts of laughter. Although he had been a slave as long as he could remember, Cleon felt sure he could play that game. It would not take long to learn, if the boys showed him how.

Cleon knew he must get back to his copying. But all he could think of was the group of boys having fun in the courtyard.

Cleon touched the good-luck charm he wore beneath his tunic. "O Artemis," he prayed, "please let me get to know them. Please let me have friends!" Why did she not answer his prayers? Was he always to be lonely and afraid of a cruel master who flogged him?

Before he could stop himself, a sob shook Cleon's body; tears filled his eyes. A tear fell onto the papyrus. It blurred the ink at the bottom of the page. Cleon did not hear the sound behind him. He did not see Marcus Vitruvius, his master, standing in the doorway of the library, fanning himself with a huge fan.

Cleon wiped his eyes on his sleeve and picked up the sponge eraser to correct the mistake. But he was too late.

"Slave! You shall be flogged for this!" Vitruvius screamed. His short, thick body shook with rage. He grabbed the sponge from Cleon's hand and wiped the entire page clean.

"But it was only one mistake," Cleon said. "Now I'll have to do it all over!"

"You'll not talk back to me, slave!" Vitruvius strode back and forth in rage. His beady eyes became slits. "I have sworn to own the largest library in the empire! No one will stop me! Least of all, one of my own possessions!" He spat out the words with scorn.

Hatred filled Cleon's heart. He tried to turn away, but Vitruvius picked up the reed pen and, in a fury of anger, scratched its sharp point across Cleon's face. "Thing! Dog!" he yelled. "Out into the courtyard with you! I'll have you flogged. And just in case someone else gets the smart idea to defy me, I'll gather an audience so that they can benefit by this example!"

On the street, Cleon stopped running. It was hot and crowded. Pentecost, the spring festival of the harvest, had just been celebrated. From all over Palestine, travelers still milled inside the walls of the Holy City.

Cleon looked around frantically. He must not act as though he were escaping. A row of shops lined the street. He slipped through the crowds past the grocery store and headed for the export shop where Alexander, his friend, was the shopkeeper. Alexander belonged to a friend of Vitruvius, and he and Cleon had been sold at the same auction. Surely Alexander would help him!

Cleon opened the door quickly, for he could already hear Vitruvius' shouts in the distance. Luckily, no one was in the shop except Alexander.

"Please, Alexander, help me!" Cleon begged. "I pray the gods you will help me. Vitruvius is angry with me and will flog me. Please hide me!"

The shouting had reached the lower courtyard. It was coming closer.

Alexander took one look at the boy. "You take a

big chance coming here," he said. "Good for you, it's almost noontime. The shop might have been full." He motioned for Cleon to hide behind one of the packing boxes in the rear of the shop.

They heard a commotion outside on the street. Cleon hardly dared to breathe. If they found him hiding here, Alexander too would be flogged. Cleon made himself as small as possible behind the large crate. He shivered as he heard running feet and the shouts of men on the street. A sickening, lonesome feeling came over him.

The noises outside stopped. Cleon held his breath.

"Cleon," he heard Alexander whisper. Was Alexander going to turn him back to Vitruvius?

"They have gone to the north," his friend said. "Come."

Cleon crawled out. His legs were stiff and shaky. The wound on his face had stopped bleeding, but his white tunic was soiled.

"Now, tell me, what has happened?" asked Alexander.

Cleon told him in a few words.

"You put me in grave danger," Alexander said. He handed Cleon a clean tunic to wear over his own. "You cannot stay here. You'll have to leave. I'll pray the gods to help you."

There was a sound outside on the street. Cleon jumped quickly behind the boxes again. The door opened, and a boy Cleon's own age came in.

"Hello," the boy said to Alexander. He spoke in Greek, but from his long, black hair, Cleon knew he was a Jew.

"Do you have any knucklebones for sale?"

"No," Alexander answered shortly.

Cleon saw the boy look around. He seemed to be in no hurry. His eyes were a deep brown, almost black. His face was sunbrowned. He wore a short-sleeved linen garment, bound around the waist with a bright-blue girdle.

"You could try the butcher shop," Alexander said.

The boy laughed. "But I want special knucklebones, carved or painted ones. You have all kinds of things here, and I was sure . . ."

Alexander lost his fright and breathed easier. He was a gentle man and wanted trouble from no one. "Boy," he said, "I have exports from Iberia, India—anywhere you mention—but I do not have knucklebones."

"That's all right, sir. I just wanted something to do," the boy said. "I'll look around. My father and I are from Caesarea. We don't know anybody here in Jerusalem. I mean, the only place I've been to is the temple. My name is David," he said, and smiled.

Cleon watched the boy walk around, touch, sniff, feel everything. Once he stepped dangerously close to Cleon's hiding place.

"Don't you want some game or toy?" Alexander asked sharply. "Come back tomorrow if all you want to do is look around. It's almost noon, and I'm ready to close." He walked toward the back of the shop and into the courtyard, hoping to discourage the young customer.

Cleon felt a desperate longing to talk to David. Maybe the boy would help him escape. But that was foolish! David was a Jew and Cleon a Gentile. Anyway, what could David do? "But, if only I could just talk with him," Cleon thought again.

David left the shop. With sudden impulse, Cleon followed him out to the street. Although it was nearly noon, there were still plenty of people about. Cleon did not want to frighten the boy. It could be dangerous. What if David shouted, "A slave! Here is a slave!" Still, Cleon knew he could not stay with Alexander. What did he have to lose?

Quickly, Cleon reached into his tunic and brought out his good-luck charm. It was a pair of brightly painted knucklebones.

2

Cleon ran up to David. "Here," he said quickly, shoving the gift into the boy's hand. "You can have them for keeps."

"Thanks," David said. "Why, this is just what I wanted. How did you know?" He smiled broadly at Cleon, then stared at Cleon's short red hair and blue eyes. He noticed the jagged cut on Cleon's cheek.

"You're hurt!" David exclaimed. "What happened?"

Then he saw the chain hanging from Cleon's neck—the chain that only slaves wore. David's eyes widened.

"Please keep walking," Cleon said. "I'll tell you everything."

"All right. Come on," David said.

Cleon's head turned nervously from side to side as he talked. He knew David trusted him, but perhaps Vitruvius was just ahead of them—or just behind.

Soon they were near the temple. Cleon told his story, and the two boys walked in silence for a while.

"My name's David. What's yours?"

"Cleon."

A group of men came toward them. They were talking excitedly and making wide gestures with their hands. Cleon started to run.

David grabbed him. "Don't run away!" he exclaimed. "I won't tell. I'll help you. Let's go into the temple and figure out what to do."

"But I can't go to the temple." Cleon drew back. "I'm a Gentile. Only Jews can go to the temple. There's a death penalty for anyone else."

"You can go as far as the court of the Gentiles," David said. "You'll be safer in there than you are out here. It's always full of people. No one will even notice you because they'll be too busy. Come on. We can go into the court of the Gentiles or even on Solomon's porch."

But still Cleon hung back. "I don't look like you," he said. "My hair is short and combed differently. . . ." He fingered the tag hanging on his slave chain. "Someone would be sure to recognize me."

"Then we'll disguise you right now," David answered.

The boys stepped up close to the wall.

David took off the scarf that was folded around his neck to keep his collar clean. It was a piece of silk about a yard square. Folding it diagonally, he put it onto Cleon's head. He covered Cleon's cheekbones and the back of his neck. Then he draped it so that Cleon's eyes were screened a little. David reached into his tunic top, pulled out a piece of braided cord, and wound it around Cleon's head.

"Boys don't have to wear this," David said, stepping back to admire his handiwork, "but you're taller than I am, and it looks fine. Your master will never recognize you now! Come on!"

As Cleon followed his new friend, he noticed the tall spikes on top of the wall. The two boys walked into a large courtyard. There were smaller courts and porches fenced by columns on every side. Cleon looked around with awe. He had heard much about the temple. It was more exciting and more beautiful than he had imagined.

Straight ahead was a T-shaped sanctuary with a large porch. "The holy of holies is in there," David said. "No one but the high priest is allowed to enter."

"What's inside it?" Cleon asked, remembering the sanctuaries of pagan temples that were filled with beautiful statues and splendid jewels.

"Why, nothing," David answered. "I mean, God is in there." He stopped.

Cleon looked puzzled.

In the next courtyard, priests were busy preparing animals for sacrifice. Eight marble slabs held the offerings. Farther away, a series of rings held animals that had not yet been slain. Cleon watched with wide-open eyes. Everybody was busy. No one noticed the boys.

"We'd better get that tag off your neck," David said, leading Cleon toward a huge column. Again he reached into his tunic and this time pulled out a sharpened piece of iron. "It's a cutter," he said proudly. "I found it this morning. I—I tried it on my face. It's sharp. I think I can use it to pry apart a link of the chain." He found a link weaker than the others and began to pry at it.

The prying hurt, but Cleon bit his lip and did not say a word. Finally, the chain snapped. Cleon rubbed his neck. He had worn that chain for many years. Links had been added as he grew, but not once had he been without it.

"Now, what are you going to do?" Cleon asked.

"I don't know," David answered thoughtfully. "I'd like to take you back to my father. But—"

Cleon nodded miserably. He had forgotten for a minute that he was a Gentile and David a Jew. "If only I could get outside Jerusalem," he said, "maybe I could find work."

David said, "You could pretend you are a Jewish slave who was just freed. I don't think anyone would question you."

"But how am I going to get outside the wall?" Cleon asked. "Vitruvius probably has guards at every gate."

"I've got it!" David cried excitedly. "I know just what to do!"

But before he could explain, a noisy, violent mob surged into the courtyard and ran up on the steps of Solomon's porch. Cleon and David had to jump back quickly to get out of the way.

"Where is he?" someone yelled. "Where is this man who has defiled our holy place?"

The air was full of angry shouts and threats. More men joined the mob; and, in a few minutes, the angry group came toward the boys again. "We've got him! This is the man who is teaching against the Law!" someone cried.

"Kill him! Stone him!"

"Dog! Traitor! Blasphemer!"

The shouts grew louder and louder. Cleon and David were swept out of the temple area with the angry mob. Cleon trembled. He could not see who was being dragged away, but he felt as if it were himself.

"What do you suppose he did?" Cleon asked David.

"Probably someone from that new sect," David answered. "They call themselves followers of the Way, or Christians. My father says they're trying to divide us. He used to call them blasphemers. But since we've been in Jerusalem—" David shrugged his shoulders. "You wouldn't understand," he said.

"I wonder if they're going to stone him," David said when he caught his breath again.

"Maybe they'll send him to the gladiatorial school and throw him into the arena," Cleon answered. He tried to keep close to David in the crowd. "That's what sometimes happens to us slaves."

Just then a tribune appeared and tried to calm the angry people. David and Cleon heard him shouting orders to a centurion. "Put this man in chains before the crowd takes the law into its own hands!" the tribune shouted. Then he turned to the people. "Now, what did this man do?"

Everyone spoke at once. David and Cleon could not understand a word. Neither could the tribune.

"Take him to the barracks," he ordered the centurion.

The crowd followed the soldiers. They pushed and shoved and shouted. Again David and Cleon were pushed along. Once Cleon fell down. When he managed to get up, the mob had thinned a little. The people had quieted down.

"What should we do?" Cleon asked David. "What was the plan you were going to tell me?"

There was no answer.

Cleon looked around wildly. David was nowhere in sight!

3

"It would have been better if I hadn't met David," Cleon thought miserably as he watched the angry faces of the people. Now he felt twice as frightened as before. David probably did not like him. He had probably planned it this way all along. David wanted nothing to do with a runaway slave.

Cleon walked along slowly. He felt safe enough now, but what difference did it make? His master would catch up with him sooner or later. He felt a hand on his arm and jumped quickly.

It was David! "Oh, am I glad I found you!" David exclaimed. "We were separated by the crowd. I thought you were right beside me!"

For the first time in a long while, Cleon smiled. David did like him after all!

"Come on," David said, taking his friend's arm. "You can hide in the stable back of the inn where my father and I are staying. It isn't used any more. No one will ever find you. I'll bring you something to eat every day."

"But I can't stay there forever," Cleon said. "I'd die there maybe."

"No you won't. It'll be only for a few days. We're leaving for home—for Caesarea soon. Father is taking some carts back with him. You can hide in one of them until we get through the gates! I've been thinking it all out." David was excited.

The more the boys discussed the idea, the better it sounded to them. Cleon's face was beginning to hurt again, but he tried not to show it. They walked to the inn and around behind it to the empty stable. No one was in sight, but still they crept in carefully.

It was more like a storage place for junk than a stable. They found a corner where Cleon could hide, in case anyone should happen to come by unexpectedly. Then they gathered up loose straw for a bed. The stable was dirty and dusty, but a part of one wall was open to let in light and air.

David cleared a space on the floor and sat down. "When we're outside the gates, you can walk to Caesarea with us. Father might know of someone who would hire you. He might even hire you himself."

Cleon looked at his friend shyly. "I will pray the gods for that to happen," he said.

David jumped up. "You'll have to stop talking like that!" he exclaimed. "You'll have to forget all about being a heathen if you expect to fool anybody."

"But I don't know anything else," Cleon said humbly.

"Then I'll teach you," David answered. He sat down again. "If you're going to pretend you're one of us, you'll have to believe with all your heart that there is only one God."

"You mean one God can take care of everything?"

"Everything and everybody," David answered and looked at Cleon closely. "Say—it will help that your clothes look like ours. Caesarea has many Romans and Greeks. But maybe I ought to get one of Father's prayer shawls for you, just in case."

"All right." Cleon smiled. He did not know what a prayer shawl was, but he was willing to do anything for his new friend.

"I'll get something for you to eat, and then we can talk," David said, and left.

Cleon huddled in his corner. He felt a little better. He had a friend, and the friend wanted to help him.

David came back soon with some bread and fruit. "I've decided you don't need the prayer shawl," he said as he handed a pear to Cleon. "You'll look all right anyway. All you need to know is the right words to say." Both boys started to eat.

"I'd like to live in Caesarea with you, David," Cleon said. "But you'd better tell me more about your God so that I can sound more like you."

David chewed on his pear and tried to explain about there being only one God. "You know what!" he exclaimed. "You could become a proselyte."

"What's that?" Cleon asked.

"Why—why, a proselyte is a convert. It's someone who wasn't born a Jew but who has become one," David explained.

"Oh, I'd like that," Cleon said. "I'd like to be like you. But what do I have to do?"

"You go to the synagogue school and study. You can go with me. Then later you will be able to go to the synagogue itself." David looked at Cleon. "Maybe you'd better get permission. Is your father a slave too?"

Cleon shrugged. "I guess he was, but I don't know. I'm an orphan. No one would care what I became."

"That's too bad." David's voice was full of sympathy.

Cleon smiled a little. "I had a good teacher before Marcus Vitruvius bought me. My teacher was a slave too, and he liked me. He taught me mathematics and grammar. I know how to parse a sentence!"

David looked at Cleon with wonder. "You're smart," he said. "You could teach me a lot of things!"

The boys finished eating. Their fingers pulled at pieces of straw; then the boys matched lengths.

"What's your father like?" Cleon asked.

"He's a merchant. He buys all kinds of handwork in the villages to sell in the city. Then he takes things from the city back to the villages. This is the first time I ever came with him to Jerusalem."

"I mean, what's he like inside? Will he be angry if he finds me hiding in one of his carts?"

"Oh, he'll never know! He's always talking business. Don't worry about him!" David paused; he looked worried himself.

Cleon noticed it. "But you are worried," he said.

"Well-ll," David confided, "I'm worried, but not about you. It's Father. He's been acting strangely lately. He's a Pharisee, and that means he has studied all the laws." David scowled. "But now he seems to be interested in this new sect."

"What's strange about that?"

"Well, you saw them drag that man from the temple today. It's dangerous! Those people say that the Messiah has already come."

"Who's the Messiah?"

"A King whom God is going to send someday. Somebody is always claiming to be the Messiah, just to get people to follow him."

"But if your father knows that—"

"But this One is different. His name is Jesus. He died a long time ago, when Father was a little boy, and people are still following what He said! Every day, more and more people become Christians. That's what the sect is called."

"Do you think your Father will join?" Cleon asked.

"No," David answered. "I really don't think Father believes that Jesus is the Messiah, but he keeps asking everybody many questions. And he's stopped calling the Christians blasphemers."

4

Cleon did not quite understand, but he was so anxious to please his new friend that he nodded eagerly. He wanted David to keep right on talking. There was much to learn.

David jumped up. “I’ve got to go,” he said. “Father will be here soon. Maybe I can come back later.” He frowned. “That’s another thing,” he said almost in a whisper. “Father’s been going out every night. I don’t know where. I tried to follow him once, but I was afraid I’d become lost. I’ll come out here tonight if he leaves again.”

Cleon settled back into the straw. He thought over

the things David had told him. "One God. There is only one God." He must say it over and over until he believed it. "To worship God is to love Him." That seemed strange. How could you love someone you could not see?

"David said you start out by saying special words. 'Holy, holy, holy, Lord God of Hosts!' But what do they mean? I must remember to ask David." He was becoming drowsy. Maybe he'd become a proselyte . . . and be almost . . . like David. . . .

Cleon fell asleep. He dreamed he was in Caesarea with David. In his dream, they were going to the synagogue, arm in arm.

Meanwhile, inside a small restaurant adjoining the inn, David sat with his father. It was dark and small. There were only a few tables.

Absalom, David's father, seemed deep in his own thoughts. He was not a handsome man, but he attracted attention everywhere. He was a man of average height, with straight shoulders and a firm step. His face was finely molded, his forehead high, and his jaw square cut. David knew that his father was a just man, but a hard one.

David stuffed some fruit and grain cakes inside his tunic for Cleon. He wished he could talk to his father—really talk. Absalom was always busy defending and upholding the Law.

"Father," David asked suddenly, "what's the best way to heal a wound?"

"What kind of wound?" Absalom asked.

David put his hand to his cheek, then withdrew it quickly. "Well, sort of a cut. It isn't bleeding any more. I mean a cut that has stopped bleeding."

"It needs to be washed out," his father said. "There is always the danger of infection. Vinegar should be used."

"Thank you, Father." David was silent for a minute.

"Father?"

"Yes, Son."

"I have another question. What would you do if you met a runaway slave?"

Absalom looked at David quickly. "A slave is his master's property. I would return him immediately."

"Even if you knew his master would flog him or—or send him to the gladiatorial school?"

"It's not my business what his master does with him," said Absalom

David looked away. One minute his father was very kind; then, all of a sudden, he changed.

The innkeeper walked toward them with more food. He winked knowingly at Absalom. "They have one of the leaders of the new sect in prison," he said. "I heard they dragged him from the temple this afternoon!"

Absalom stared at the innkeeper without seeing him. David stuffed another cake in his tunic.

"Blasphemer!" continued the innkeeper. "If the powers that be aren't strong enough to defend the temple from such teaching, it's high time we take matters into our own hands!"

"But they were going to stone him," Absalom said quietly. "The soldiers had to protect him. I heard him speak just a short while before. Paul is his name. He is a very learned man."

The innkeeper laughed. "You have been coming here for many years, Absalom. Don't tell me you're defending those profane people! You should have thrown the first stone!"

Absalom looked away. He seemed uneasy. David watched with amazement. Was his father defending the new sect?

"If it is just another group of fanatics, it will soon die," Absalom said. "But if it is the truth, then we would be opposing God's will."

"But to admit Gentiles to our faith without making them keep the Law!" The innkeeper picked up his tray and moved off. They could hear him mumbling,

"I wish I had been there! I would have put a stop to that nonsense!"

"Father," David asked after a while, "what is a gladiatorial school?"

"Why so many questions today?" Absalom was watching the innkeeper. "It's a school where gladiators are trained for the fights in the arena. They are usually prisoners or public enemies."

"Or—runaway slaves?" David asked hesitantly.

"Why all this interest in runaway slaves?" Absalom asked. He looked sharply at his son.

"I—I just wondered," David answered, hoping he had not said too much. It was useless to ask his father for help. "I—I saw a boy about my age today. He was running from something. I felt sorry for him."

"It is well known that some slaves are cruelly treated, but it is not our business nor responsibility," Absalom said. "We can only pity them."

They finished supper. As they entered their room, David stopped. "It's too hot to sleep right now. I guess I'll go for a walk."

"No," Absalom said. "The streets are not safe for a young boy at night."

"I won't go far," David begged. He wished his father would stop treating him like a baby. His father went out every night. Why could he not take a little walk?

But Absalom refused to allow David to leave the room. David knew he would have to wait until his father went out. He lay down on one of the thin mattresses and pretended to fall asleep. He had to be careful to keep the food he had hidden in his tunic from spilling.

Finally, Absalom left, and David sneaked out to the stable. He could not get the vinegar tonight. That would have to wait until tomorrow.

"I can't stay," David said breathlessly to Cleon. "Here." He gave Cleon the food.

Cleon was holding his face in pain. He bit his lip to keep from showing how much it hurt. He took the food David offered him, but he was not hungry.

When David left, Cleon settled back on the straw again. The moon shone through the open space in the wall. It made long, frightening shadows. Cleon had never felt so lonely in his life. He had given away his good-luck piece. He felt he could no longer call on his old gods to help him. He still did not know how to pray to the new God about whom David had told him.

5

When Cleon awoke the next day, the sun was straight above the stable. David was sitting beside him.

"I thought you'd never wake up!" David said. "I've been out here three times already. Look what I've got for you."

David picked up a jar of wine and poured some on a piece of cloth. "That cut looks pretty bad. I asked Father how to heal it. He said to wash it with vinegar. I couldn't get any; so I brought wine."

Cleon held the cloth to his face. When the stinging finally stopped, the cut felt better. "I'm hungry now," Cleon said. He still felt as if he were dreaming.

David produced more dates, figs, and cakes from his tunic. "I had a hard time getting these," he said. "Father is suspicious. He watches every move I make. I thought he would never leave for the market today." David sat down beside Cleon.

Both boys ate in silence for a while; then David said, "It's just like our cave at home, where the gang meets." He looked around the stable. "I mean, the straw and the way it's somewhat hidden."

"Do you play games in the cave?" Cleon asked.

"Sometimes. Mostly, we play things like pirates or soldiers." David laughed as he remembered.

"Do all the boys in Caesarea belong?" Cleon asked.

"Oh, no! Only a few who go to the synagogue school—my special friends. We have a password. You can't tell anyone what it is because only the boys who know it can get in. We don't ask just everybody to join—only those we want." David looked proud.

Cleon remembered the group of boys playing in the courtyard under the window that last day he had worked in Vitruvius' library. Maybe they had a cave and a secret password too. Would David ask him to join the gang when they arrived at Caesarea?

"We don't allow girls," David continued. "It makes my sister, Rebecca, mad. She's always following us around. She's a pest."

"I don't have any brothers or sisters," Cleon said, "and I don't even remember my mother." He was silent for a moment. Then he said, "You'd better tell me some more about your religion." He would never be accepted by David's friends and know the password if he did not learn much more.

"That's right," David said. "I'll tell you about the prophets. They're important. You know, Moses, Isaiah . . ."

The two boys talked on. Cleon's eagerness made him a good student. Besides, when he thought about something else, his face did not hurt so much.

David did not come to the stable all the next day. When he did arrive, Cleon knew his friend was in trouble. David did not say much and he frowned often.

Finally, Cleon asked, "What's the matter, David? Is it your father again?"

David nodded. "He was gone nearly all night. He brought a man home with him, and they talked about the new sect until morning. I couldn't leave today because Father didn't go to the market."

Cleon could not understand why his friend was so upset. "I don't see what difference it makes," he said. "Maybe the new sect is all right."

"Well, you don't know my family. And Father

seems very unhappy—mixed up, as though he can't quite make up his mind."

"Maybe they've cast a spell on him," Cleon said.

"I don't believe in spells, but that's the way he acts," David said. "If only I knew what was going on!"

Cleon wanted to help his friend. After all, David had helped him. But what could he do? Suddenly, Cleon felt hot and dizzy. He slumped down on the straw. His cheek throbbed and his mind was buzzing. "I feel very warm," he said weakly. "I wish we could walk outside."

"Yes, the air is bad in here," David agreed. He looked out of the opening. It was almost dark. "Father went away just a few minutes ago," he said. "I don't think it will be dangerous if we walk around a little. If we stay close together, no one will notice us."

The two boys walked quietly out of the stable and onto the street. They walked down one narrow street and then another. The moon cast their shadows straight ahead of them. Cleon sucked in the fresh air. It made him feel better.

All at once, David stopped walking. "There's Father!" he said. "Ahead of us! Let's follow him!"

There were other people on the street, but the boys had no trouble trailing Absalom's erect figure and firm, determined step. Once, when he turned a corner, they nearly lost him. They saw Absalom stop and look around. David grabbed Cleon and pulled him into the shadows. When David saw his father start out again, he motioned Cleon to follow. Soon they saw a group of houses built close together. They were all alike, just big boxes with flat rooftops.

They saw Absalom go up to one of the houses and knock on the door. The boys crept as close as possible without being seen.

"I wonder what Father is doing in this poor neighborhood," David whispered.

"There are steps leading to the roof. Let's go up," Cleon suggested.

They went up the steps quickly and quietly. The roof was made of rough rafters, over which branches had been laced. Wet mud had been used to plaster it. The mud had baked hard in the sun, but it was crumbly in places. The boys had to be careful.

A faint glimmer of light shone through the roof where the branches had loosened. Absalom was directly beneath them in a room full of men and women. They were all talking and laughing. Cleon noticed that there were different levels around the sides of the room. One seemed to be the kitchen, another a place for sleeping. He had never seen a house like that before.

A man handed Absalom a letter. "We would appreciate it, Brother Absalom, if you would deliver this to the brethren at Caesarea."

Absalom nodded and put the letter into his tunic. A hush fell over everyone. The boys saw another man get up and turn to face the group. He spoke about Jesus Christ. He told the people how Jesus had fulfilled the prophecies of the Scriptures. "Jesus performed many miracles among us," he said. "He healed the sick. He brought the dead back to life. After he was crucified, He rose from the dead that we, through Him, might have eternal life."

"A man was really raised from the dead?" Cleon asked in wonder.

"Sh-h-h!" David said. "There's Father. He's going to say something!"

Cleon leaned down to get a better look. At that instant a twig broke from one of the branches and fell through the opening. Everyone looked up. The two boys darted down the steps. They ran down the narrow streets back to the stable without speaking a word.

Inside the stable, Cleon pressed his hand against his cheek. It hurt more than ever and felt twice as big. But he must not think about it. Now, he must try to remember what he had just seen and heard.

"Your father . . ." he started slowly. "Your . . . father seems to have made up his mind. He . . . he seems to be one of them." The pain was filling his head.

"Maybe it's a trick to catch them," David said.

Cleon's tongue was dry. "You mean he took the letter . . . so he can find out where the Christians meet in Caesarea . . . and trap them?"

"Maybe," David said, "but no—that can't be it because Father already knows where they meet. It just doesn't seem possible that he finally believes Jesus is the Messiah. How can he?"

"Why not?" Cleon pressed his hand harder to his hot cheek. "I didn't find it so hard to believe in just one God, your God," he reminded his friend.

"That's different," David said.

Cleon's thoughts began to wander. If only he did not feel so hot! Cleon liked Absalom, from what he had seen and heard. What was David saying? He could not quite hear the words.

"Father not only talks about Jesus but keeps talking about a Spirit who will lead him," David said. "Now, what do you think that . . . ?"

David stopped when he saw Cleon stumble to the wall and lean against it limply. He put his hand to Cleon's forehead. It was burning. Even by moonlight, David could see that Cleon's face was flushed and swollen. "You've got a fever," he said. "You need help. I'll get Father. I hope he has come back," David said, and ran out.

How long he lay there, Cleon was not sure. He was dizzy with pain and fever. Suddenly, the room came alive with light. Roman soldiers with huge torches circled the stable. Cleon lay very still.

"We'll find him!" a soldier shouted. "If he's still in Jerusalem, we'll find him!"

6

David ran quickly from the stable to the room at the inn, half fearful that his father would not have returned. But when he opened the door, he saw Absalom studying an open scroll. He did not look up as David came in.

"Father," David pleaded, "you've got to help us. Quick!"

"David! I've been waiting for you. I must talk to you, my son."

"There isn't time now, Father. A friend of mine is hurt. He has a cut on his face and it's infected. He has a fever." David was frantic.

"Where is he?" Absalom rose from his chair.

"In the stable back of the inn. Hurry, Father." David looked out the window. He saw the torches of Roman soldiers. They were marching down the street. He could hear them shouting in the distance.

Absalom followed David down the stairs, through the courtyard, and into the stable. "We're here," David called to Cleon. "Father is going to help you!"

There was no answer.

David began to push aside the scraps and rubbish. He looked through the straw. There was not a sign of Cleon anywhere. "Father, they've found him! We've got to go after him!"

"Who has found whom?" asked Absalom.

"The soldiers! I just saw them go down the street. They must have been here, searching around the stable. Maybe they were looking for Cleon. Maybe his master sent them."

"What are you talking about?" Absalom asked. "This stable has been deserted for many years. It's a part of the soldier's duty to search empty buildings."

"But this is different, Father. You don't understand. Please, help me save my friend," David begged.

Absalom followed his son out of the stable. They crossed the street and started after the soldiers.

"What is a friend of yours doing in a stable?" Absalom asked.

David stopped and looked at his father. His eyes pleaded for understanding. "Father," he said, "I have a confession to make. I have been hiding a runaway slave. He has a cruel master. Father, we've got to help him. If we don't, he may be sent to the arena. Anyway, he'll be flogged. I know he will."

"We can't take him from the soldiers," Absalom answered. "We can't become involved in this, Son."

"But maybe the soldiers don't have him." David pulled at his father's arm, forcing him up the street. "Maybe he ran away when he saw their torches."

"We have no business interfering," Absalom said, but he followed David's anxious feet.

The soldiers disappeared around a corner. David and Absalom hurried after. Just then, three men came from between two houses. They were dragging a young boy behind them. One of the men held a lantern to his face. "It's the quaestor's scribe," he said. "I'd swear to it!"

"No," David yelled, running up to the boy lying on the street. "We're here! Father and I are here!"

The three men stepped back; and Absalom, with a quick movement, bent over the young boy. "My son," he said gently, "you are sick. Why did you run away?"

"Is this your boy?" asked one of the men.

Absalom stooped and picked up Cleon into his arms.

"I told you you were wrong," the second man said. "This is a sick Jew. Even Marcus Vitruvius would find no sport in flogging him!" He turned to Absalom. "We beg your pardon, sir. We meant no harm. We were passing by and heard someone moaning. The boy was delirious. We meant to help him."

The three men bowed and moved off down the street.

Absalom carried Cleon back to the inn. He laid the unconscious boy on one of the pallets and washed out his wound. Then he took vinegar and cleansed it. He forced liquid through Cleon's lips. David watched, helping where he could.

Cleon said nothing. His head lay back. His cheek was inflamed and swollen. He had not even opened his eyes.

When Absalom finished, he and David sat at the other end of the room. "Is he all right, Father?" David asked. "He looks very sick."

"It will take time for the fever to pass, but he will be all right," Absalom answered. He looked at the boy lying on the couch. His headdress had slipped off, revealing the short, red hair.

"He's a Gentile!" Absalom said, shocked.

"You won't throw him out, will you?" David asked in fright.

"N-no," Absalom answered, "but, David, tell me again what happened."

When David finished, Absalom said to his son, "Try to get some sleep. It's late. We leave for home tomorrow."

"What about Cleon? Can we take him with us?"

"We'll talk about it in the morning," Absalom answered and sat down to watch beside the sick boy.

David slept fitfully that night. Every time he opened his eyes, he saw his father still sitting beside Cleon. There was a look on Absalom's face that David had never seen before. It was a look of love, but it was also as if he had heard some good news. Finally, David slept.

In the morning, David found Cleon sitting up. His cheek was no longer swollen, and he was smiling. Absalom was not in the room. "Whew!" David breathed. "You gave us a scare last night!"

Cleon's smile broadened. "Your father is a good man," he said. "That stuff he put on my face hurt, but I didn't want to tell him. Look, it's better."

"Where is Father now?" David asked. He stood up and stretched.

"I don't know. He wasn't here when I woke up. Hey, look at the sun! It must be nearly noon."

Absalom had left food on the table. The two boys began to eat. "Do you think your father will help me get out of Jerusalem?" asked Cleon.

"I don't know. I told you he seems different, somehow. I don't know what to expect."

Cleon remembered the torches of the night before. "You don't think he went to my master?"

"I don't know. I really don't."

"I like your father," Cleon admitted frankly. "He made me well. I hope he likes me."

The door opened and Absalom came in. He gave David an affectionate pat, and walked directly to Cleon. He examined his face and felt his forehead, nodding approval. "It looks fine," he said. "If only I had seen it sooner, we might have prevented the scar. But it will be fine."

"I tried to ask you for help, Father," David said, "but I knew . . ."

"I know, Son, I know," Absalom said. "But now I have learned that the Son of God changes men and makes all things new. Life is different for me now. We'll talk about it on the way home."

David jumped up. "Are we taking Cleon with us?"

Cleon said eagerly, "I am well educated. I can

write and speak three languages. I will be your slave."

"I have no need of slaves, my boy," Absalom said, "but I can always use another son."

Tears came to Cleon's eyes. "Thank you, sir," David said. "Thank you."

"I've explained about our God to him," David said. "He isn't a heathen any more."

"Yes, David says maybe I can be a proselyte—"

"Just a minute, boys, just a minute!" Absalom raised his hand to quiet the excited pair. "I have said good-by to my new friends here. Now I must go to Vitruvius and see if he will sell you to me."

Cleon's face fell. "I am useful to my master. He may not want to sell me."

"Father, must you go to him? If he won't sell Cleon, he'll punish him even more than he had planned."

Absalom put an arm about each boy. "I will do everything in my power to buy Cleon. But he is another man's property, and I cannot take him nor shield him without disobeying the law."

Absalom made the boys promise to stay at the inn until he finished his business.

7

Cleon was frightened as he watched the door close behind Absalom. "It's no use. I know it won't do any good," he said. "All the money in the world wouldn't please my master half so much as flogging me and making me work harder."

David tried to cheer him. "Father will think of something. Let's talk about what we're going to do when we get home." Suddenly David stopped. "I wonder if Father really is a Christian. If he is, people will make fun of him and torment him." He sighed. "Maybe they'll stone him. Anyway, I'm not sure I want my father to be a Christian."

"Do you know what a Christian really is?" Cleon asked.

"No, but I'm going to find out. Maybe we can get him to change his mind on the road to Caesarea—before we reach home."

"But, David," Cleon argued, "maybe there's nothing we can do about it. Maybe your father isn't afraid that people will make fun of him or—or even stone him!" He paused and thought a moment. "I know one thing, David; I don't think I'd want to worship my old gods again, now that you've told me about your God."

Before David could answer, Absalom returned. "Vitruvius has gone," he said. "No one knows where. He was sent away suddenly. His household has gone with him. The apartment is empty."

The two boys looked at each other and wide grins spread across their faces. Then they sighed with relief.

"I can take you home with me now with a clear conscience, for I have done what I could," Absalom said. "But if we ever hear where your master is, Cleon, we must go to him."

Now that it had happened, Cleon could find no words. He was to have a family, at last. He was going to belong to someone who cared about him. It was more than he had hoped for! And maybe they would never find Vitruvius. Of course, they hoped they would not. Probably he had been sent back to Rome. Cleon's thoughts were full of hope.

"The carts are ready," Absalom told the boys. "We should reach Bethel by nightfall. Then we will go on to Samaria."

Absalom's carts were loaded and waiting. He had hired a man to take care of the oxen. The procession moved slowly toward the gates of the city. Cleon walked between Absalom and David. He did not look back until they passed the outer wall.

The road to Caesarea was filled with travelers and carts. The route led north, down from the rocky hills of Jerusalem, through rich green valleys and fertile farmland. It was level part of the way, but the road often wound over stony hills before disappearing into sprawling vineyards or bursting olive orchards.

Absalom joined a fellow traveler just outside the city walls. They walked beside the carts, talking, talking, talking.

The two boys ran ahead on the hot, dusty road. They tried to see who could throw rocks the farthest.

"It was much nicer when we came to Jerusalem," David told Cleon. "There were all kinds of flowers then."

"Are there always so many people walking?" asked Cleon. This was his first trip through the country on foot. Before, traveling with Vitruvius and other masters, he had gone by sea in high-masted merchant ships or as a part of a large caravan. He still could not believe the wonderful thing that had happened to him.

"There are more people at Passover time. And look at Father! Still talking about that new sect with everyone he meets! He used to talk only business, and he was always in such a hurry to get somewhere!"

"He's talking with the same man we met just outside the city," Cleon said. "Didn't he call himself an evangelist? What's that?"

"I think it's the same as a traveling storyteller, except that an evangelist tells only good news."

"I heard him say the Name Jesus. That's the Man we heard about the other night, isn't it? Who is He? I don't understand Him very well."

"I told you, Cleon. He's some kind of Prophet, I think. There's always someone claiming to be the Messiah."

"Who did you say the Messiah is?" Cleon pulled at his headdress. It bothered him.

"The Messiah is a King who will be sent by God to rule the Jews with kindness and to get rid of our enemies."

"I hope He'll get rid of my master!" Cleon said bitterly. He hated Vitruvius more than ever.

"He'll get rid of everybody who isn't one of God's chosen people," David assured Cleon.

Cleon looked startled.

"Don't worry about yourself," laughed David. "You'll become a proselyte and be a son of Israel."

The two boys walked more slowly. David kicked a pebble along with his toe. He was anxious to get home. He wondered if it would be the same as always. Would his father's new beliefs change things?

The sun beat down on them and dust was on their tongues. They found a large rock and rested in its shadow until Absalom caught up with them. The stranger was still with him. Absalom introduced the two boys.

"Let's rest for a while," Absalom said. "This man has many interesting stories to tell."

Cleon moved close to Absalom. Already he worshiped David's father, and he wanted to hear more about the Christians. If Absalom really were a Christian, then he, Cleon, would become one too! Absalom had risked his life for him. It was the least he could do to repay his debt.

But David was restless. He did not want to listen to the traveler's stories, and he wished his father would not listen. His mother would never approve. David's mother had been brought up in a Pharisee home where all the laws were strictly kept. She would never believe that the Messiah had already come, no matter what Absalom said. The closer David got toward home, the more he wanted his father to forget all his new ideas.

Besides, David was thirsty. "Come on, Cleon," he said. "Let's look for a stream or a well so that we can get a drink."

"We'll catch up with you soon," Absalom said. "Don't go too far ahead of us." He turned to the stranger. "I am anxious to hear more, for I am very new in the faith. Tell me everything!"

David led the way. There was no sign of water. "Everything has changed since we came to Jerusalem. The stream is dried up."

"Isn't there a river nearby?" Cleon asked.

"Not around here. Look!" David shouted. "A hare. Let's chase it."

The two boys left the road and raced after the animal. Laughing and shouting, they ran farther and farther from the road. When the hare hopped out of sight, Cleon stopped running.

"David," he called, "we'd better get back to your father. We're way off the highway."

"Don't worry," David said reassuringly. "We'll get back."

They turned back and could see a road down in the valley. It was lined with travelers. The boys scrambled through the rocks. "Now we'll find Father soon enough," David said.

Cleon and David caught up with the travelers, but there was no sign of Absalom. Shadows began to lengthen.

"He can't be too far ahead of us," David said. He was beginning to become worried too.

"Maybe he's behind us," Cleon said. "Maybe we ought to wait for him."

They walked up to a traveler. David asked, "Have you seen a man pass this way with two carts?" He described his father. "We are going to Bethel, and we can't find him."

"Bethel?" laughed the man. "You took the wrong turn. This is the road to Joppa!"

The two boys looked at each other. Cleon said, "We should have stayed with him."

"We'll find the road all right. Don't worry," David said. "We'll find Father before he even misses us."

They turned and ran back in the direction they had come. There were still people on the road. But when the sun set, they realized they were lost.

8

The Romans had built beautiful roads in Palestine. Footpaths blossomed into highways under the Caesars, and the highways were excellent and complicated. But Cleon and David were lost. They could not find David's father, and somehow they had missed the road to Bethel.

It was becoming dark. Most of the travelers had reached their destinations or had deserted the highway for the roadside inns. The boys began to gather up dry twigs frantically.

David looked up into the scraggly branches of a sycamore tree. He climbed it and came down with a dried-out bird's nest in one hand.

"What's that for?" Cleon asked.

"For a fire." David pulled a flint from his tunic. "Here, you want to try it?"

Cleon looked at the flint and iron curiously. He had helped tend fires. He had carried live coals in an open pan from the central hearth to light stoves and lanterns. He had even seen flame borrowed from a street lighter. But he had never seen a fire started.

David showed him how to lay the twigs and how to strike the flints together. After many attempts, Cleon was finally able to get a faint spark. It caught on to the dry nest quickly; and with much fanning and blowing, the fire flamed red.

It was completely dark now. The moon was hidden beneath a clump of trees. Cleon and David leaned over the fire. They tried not to think about the wild animals that roamed the countryside.

A faint sound reached their ears. Both boys shrank back. They knew that robbers roamed up and down the roads, looking for wealthy victims. They were afraid. The sound grew louder.

But now they could tell it was a cheerful sound—the sound of someone singing. The voices grew louder and louder. Two women and a man walked slowly toward them. They were dressed in the rough garb of Palestinian peasants.

"Don't be afraid," the man said. He had a long, flowing white beard. His voice was kind. "My name is Ezra. My companions and I would like to share our food with you in exchange for the warmth of your fire."

The women stepped forward, and Ezra introduced them as Miriam and Ruth. They smiled at Cleon and David. The boys told the strangers their names and explained what had happened to them. Soon they felt better.

"We'll all sleep here together," the old man said, "and protect each other. In the morning, I'll put you back on the road to Bethel." He sat down cross-legged, next to the fire. His eyes smiled, even though his lips did not.

"We are harvesters," Miriam told the boys. She gave each of them a pomegranate. "The crop is finished in Jericho."

"We're on our way to the plain of Sharon," Ruth said. She sat down beside Miriam. "Miriam and I are, anyway. Ezra stops in Samaria."

"Aren't you relatives?" Cleon asked. "I thought . . ."

Ezra laughed. "No, we are not relatives. We had never met until this morning. But—in one sense, yes, we are related. Miriam, Ruth, and I are followers of the Way."

"That is true. We are related," Miriam said. "We all belong to the same family. Since morning, we have been exchanging stories."

"What's a follower of the Way?" Cleon whispered to David.

David shrugged. "Another Christian, that's all—just like Father."

Ruth added a piece of wood to the fire. "Coming upon you lost boys reminds me of a story I heard the other day. Once, when our Lord was twelve years old, His parents thought He was lost. They had all gone to Jerusalem for the Passover and were returning to their home in Nazareth. They thought the Boy was with them, for there were many travelers on the road, just like today, and all were friendly and having a good time. They had gone a whole day's journey before Mary and Joseph missed their Son."

"Did they ever find Him?" Cleon asked.

"Oh, yes," Ruth answered. "His parents went back to Jerusalem. They found Him in the temple, talking with the teachers."

Miriam sighed. "How I wish I had known Him," she said. "Even at twelve, they say He had great understanding."

"Do you mean Jesus?" Cleon asked. "Is He the One you call the Messiah? The One who rose from the dead?"

"Yes," Ruth answered, "the Son of God." She reached out her hand to Ezra as though to touch his sleeve, then drew it back quickly. There was awe in her voice when she spoke again. "Ezra was in Jerusalem when our Lord ascended into heaven. Ezra talked with the apostles themselves."

"You promised to tell us more tonight," Miriam said. "Please do. O Ezra, there are not many as privileged as you!"

The old man was silent. Then he spoke softly, as though what he had to say was a great treasure.

9

Ezra told about Peter's sermons, the healing of the lame man, the many conversions in Jerusalem. Cleon felt he would never forget this night and the old man's voice coming to him across the fire.

"After Peter's first sermon," Ezra said, "three thousand men and women believed, repented, and were baptized. I know; I was one of them."

The fire had burned to embers. When Ezra stopped speaking, a new sound could be heard in the still night. It was the steady pounding of many horses' hoofs. Ezra and the two boys rose to their feet. The women moved to one side. The sound of horses and marching men grew louder and louder until what appeared to be the whole Roman army was passing slowly by. Every tenth soldier held a flare so that the whole line of march was illuminated.

The travelers hid behind a big rock. There was terror in Cleon's eyes. "You don't suppose it's my master looking for me, do you?" he asked David.

"You're not that important! Look! Here come more horsemen!"

The travelers ducked to keep from getting the dust in their eyes.

The small army passed, and the travelers stepped out from their hiding place. They stirred the fire until it was glowing again. Before they could talk about what had happened, a Roman centurion, short, red cloak slung over his shoulders, rode up on horseback. His torch had gone out, and he raked through the burning coals to relight it.

Noticing the anxious faces staring up at him, he said, "There is nothing to be alarmed about. We are taking a prisoner to Caesarea. He is not safe in Jerusalem. Forty men there have taken a vow neither to eat nor to drink until they have killed him."

"Would that be the Apostle Paul, who has been preaching in the synagogues?" Miriam inquired timidly.

"The same," answered the soldier. "A mob dragged

him from the temple recently. If you Jews don't stop rioting about this new sect, you are going to find yourselves in trouble."

Ezra shook his head sadly. "Can't they understand?" he wondered. "It's not a new sect. It's the fulfillment of the Scriptures. We are not blasphemers, as they say." Ezra went on. "We keep the Law—every letter of it! Why can't the priests and rabbis settle the question? Why must it be brought before the civil courts?"

The centurion shrugged. "We must not be talking about the same thing. This sect is open to all—Jew, Gentile, proselyte. That is the reason there are riots. Your temple is being defiled!" He sneered at Ezra.

"Who is this man called Paul?" Ezra asked. "I have been away from Jerusalem for many years and have not heard of him."

"He is a Roman citizen," answered the centurion, "and it is our duty to protect him."

"Are the forty men following you now?" asked David, and he looked back into the darkness.

"I think we gave them the slip," laughed the soldier. "Anyway, it will be the governor's headache from now on. Let Felix worry. We wash our hands of Paul!" He galloped off into the darkness, carrying the torch high above him.

Ezra seemed greatly disturbed. He kept stirring

the fire and staring into the red flames.

"Gentiles—proselytes . . ." he said and shook his head. "I am old. Is it possible Jesus will not return to restore the kingdom to Israel?"

"God's kingdom belongs to all who believe," Miriam said. "Have you not heard the story of Peter and Cornelius?"

Ezra shook his head. He kept his eyes on the woman.

"Peter had a dream," Miriam said. "In his dream, he was offered food forbidden to the Jews. Three times he refused to eat the unclean food, but a voice said, 'What God has cleansed, you must not call common.' Shortly after, he was invited to the home of Cornelius, a Gentile. Peter had never entered the house of a Gentile before, but his dream made him realize that God loves all people, Jew and Gentile. While he was telling the story of Jesus to Cornelius' household, the Holy Spirit fell upon them."

"Of course," Ezra murmured, "of course. Christ's coming was not alone to restore the kingdom of Israel. He came for every nation."

The boys watched the old man. The sadness in his face changed to reverence. "Thy will be done," he said softly. He lay down and closed his eyes. Soon he was breathing deeply.

But sleep did not come to Cleon. The Roman soldiers had terrified him. What was the use of becoming a Christian? It was no better than being a slave. The man called Paul was a prisoner. Cleon had seen him dragged from the temple, and now Paul was being pursued by forty men who had sworn to kill him. Maybe Absalom would become a prisoner too. No, Cleon decided, he would never become a Christian. There was too much danger—too much running away.

10

The next morning, the two boys, with Ezra, Miriam, and Ruth, started out early. They passed through Bethel, but there was no sign of David's father.

As they reached the northern outskirts of Bethel, a figure rushed toward them with open arms. It was Absalom. "David! Cleon!" he called.

The boys ran up to David's father. "We were lost, Father," David said breathlessly.

Absalom hugged both close to him and listened to the story of their adventures. Then he thanked the older people for their help.

Two days later, they reached Samaria. The city, renamed Sebaste by King Herod when he rebuilt it, was unusual. A triple gate opened to the main street, which had colonnades on each side. The main street and others were lined with shops, theaters, and baths. It was as much like a Roman city as Herod could make it.

Cleon and David stopped and looked into the shops. "Caesarea is like Samaria," David told Cleon, "only Caesarea is bigger."

"I can't wait to get there," Cleon said.

"We should be home in another two days," David told him. He too was becoming excited. It had been several months since he had seen his mother and his sister, Rebecca.

They continued through the city until they came to fertile farmlands on the northern outskirts. Ezra was to leave them here to stay with a friend, and Ruth and Miriam would turn off for Sharon to work in the grape harvest.

They caught up with the carts and the oxen just outside the city wall. Ezra's friend Jacob lived only a short distance away. Ezra insisted that the travelers stop to rest before continuing their journey.

A narrow footpath led to Jacob's house, which was almost like a cave, for it was built into the rocky hillside and was half hidden. Jacob was not at home; so the travelers sat down in the cool shade of a tree.

Cleon looked around. He had never seen so many trees. There were pomegranate and peach trees, fig trees and pear trees. Silver-green trees were heavy with olives. His mouth watered.

"Take all you want," Ezra said. "My friends are happy to share their fruits."

The travelers picked the fruit, ate, and rested. Just as they were ready to leave, Jacob returned. He greeted his guests and explained his absence to Ezra.

"I have been looking for help," Jacob told the old man. "Some of our harvesters are ill. Unless we get more workers, we shall lose the fig crop."

Ruth and Miriam spoke together. "We will help. We have plenty of time."

Ezra said, "I will help too." He looked apologetically at Absalom. "The crop won't wait past the Sabbath. I . . ."

"But we will help, also," Absalom put in quickly. "Won't we, boys?"

"But, Father . . ." David began. He felt embarrassed. His father, a wealthy merchant, picking figs?

Cleon asked, "May we eat as many as we want?"

Jacob laughed. "You may eat as many as you want."

There was still a whole afternoon in which to work. Everyone followed Jacob, and soon they arrived at the fig orchard. People were already scattered among the trees, picking as fast as they could. Sounds of laughter and singing rang out. Jacob showed the boys how to handle the figs to keep from bruising them. If they were bruised, they might rot before they were dried thoroughly. Jacob left the boys. Ruth and Miriam followed Jacob to another spot.

At first the boys ate more than they put into the basket. But as soon as they had eaten their fill, they were able to keep up with the others. They reached into the trees and picked the heavy, black fruit. The best figs were toward the center of the tree, high up. The boys had to reach for them.

Ezra and Absalom had taken the tree next to the boys.

"Every man and woman out there is a follower of the Way," Ezra told Absalom with delight.

"What?" Absalom sounded surprised.

"Only a few here are regular harvesters," Ezra went on. "Most are neighbors. They have other things to do, but helping Jacob save his crop is most important now."

"Are there many Christians in Samaria?" Absalom asked.

"Oh, yes. Philip, a disciple of Jesus and a great teacher, came to us from Jerusalem after the persecution." Ezra's voice trailed off as he and Absalom went to another tree.

As each basket was filled with luscious fruit, it was taken away. The figs were placed on drying trays, where they could bake in the sun for several days. Once the fruit was dry, it would keep through the winter.

David and Cleon worked hard, talking little. Finally David sat down to rest and wiped his forehead. "If we stop to help everybody we meet on the way to Caesarea, we'll never get home," he complained.

"These people stopped what they were doing to help," Cleon said thoughtfully. "They must love each other a great deal."

"I guess that proves my father really has become one of them," David said. "He certainly has changed!"

"I think he's wonderful," Cleon said shyly. "I hope I'm like him when I grow up."

"Do you want to become a Christian?"

"I'm not sure," Cleon answered. "That night when the soldiers went by with the prisoner Paul, I didn't want any part of it. But today it is different. Look what a good time we're having!"

"I'm not having a good time," David grumbled. "My arms ache and I want to get home. We'll have a good time then."

"What's your mother like?" Cleon picked up his basket again.

"She's just like Father is—or was. He's going to have a time explaining all of this to her."

"Maybe she won't like me. Maybe she won't want me to live with you," Cleon said.

"She'll do what Father wants, whether she likes it or not." David got ready to work again. "It's strange. Back in Jerusalem it all seemed so easy. But now . . ."

"Are you sorry you helped me in Jerusalem?" Cleon asked.

"Of course, I'm not sorry. But you'd better forget this new sect, and I'd better teach you more about God. What if Father should change his mind? It would be dreadful for you to be a Gentile—and a Christian!"

Cleon said uneasily, "If your father changes his mind, he won't want me around, either!"

"Don't worry about it now," David said. "If that happens, we'll just have to think of something else for you to do. You're away from your master, and that's all that counts now."

11

But Cleon could not forget so easily. Absalom was his hero. Absalom called him Son. He was a part of David's family already. He pulled a fig carefully from the tree.

David was afraid for his father. It was dangerous to belong to the new sect. But, did danger matter when everybody loved each other? The Christians here in the orchard seemed in no danger. Perhaps you had to be someone special to be in danger. Kings were in trouble half the time because someone did not like them. Maybe that was it. Maybe it was just the people who started things that got into trouble—like the man Paul.

The boys were interrupted by two, rosy-faced girls and a boy. "Hello, there," they called out, running up to David and Cleon.

"I'm Joel," the boy said, "son of Jacob, and that is Mary, my sister."

"If you climb up into the tree," Mary said to Cleon, "I'll climb after you and hold the basket. It's easier that way and faster. Joel can stand at the bottom and empty the baskets we hand down."

Cleon and Mary took one tree; David and Elizabeth another. Joel picked the lower branches, when he was not running back and forth between the pickers. It was an easy way to strip a tree, and fun too. The boys and girls laughed and talked, until it seemed that in no time at all, the sun was red in the west. The picking for that day was over.

As the boys and girls started back toward Jacob's house, where they would eat the evening meal together, Joel picked up a fig from the ground and threw it at his sister. *Plosh!* In the next second, a well-aimed shot from Elizabeth landed on his own cheek, and a fig fight was in full swing. At first David and Cleon hung back, but when they realized this was a good-natured battle, they joined the fun.

Just as quickly as the fight had begun, it was over.

The boys and girls ran to a well and washed themselves clean.

"Whew!" David gasped. "What a day this has been!"

The older people started on their way to Jacob's house, but the younger ones lagged behind. They sat down and watched the colors change in the sky. Flaming reds and golds faded into pinks and grays. One row of clouds was tinged with brown. It looked like a mountain far off from the earth.

"It's a good thing we weren't throwing stones," Elizabeth said. "You know Stephen was stoned to death."

"Who was Stephen?" Cleon asked.

"He was the first Christian martyr," Joel said. "He went all around preaching and teaching about Jesus. He explained the Scriptures and told how Jesus really was the Messiah for whom everyone had been waiting."

"But they accused him of saying bad things about God and Moses," Mary added. "That's a serious offense."

"So they stoned him," Joel said seriously. "It must have been terrible to watch. They were jealous and angry. As Stephen was dying, he asked Jesus to forgive them."

"I'm glad I wasn't there to see Stephen stoned," David said.

"But Paul was," Joel said. "His name was Saul then."

"Didn't he try to stop them from throwing stones?" Cleon asked. "If he did, maybe that's why he got into trouble."

"Paul stop them from throwing stones!" Joel exclaimed. "He didn't lift a hand to help Stephen. He was the worst persecutor of all!"

"Oh," Cleon said and smiled. "You know, at first I thought you meant another Paul. One night when we made a fire on the side of the road, hundreds of Roman soldiers passed by. They had a prisoner by the name of Paul. But that Paul is a Christian."

"It's the same man—the same Paul! He was converted," Joel said.

Cleon was excited. He turned to David. "He must be the same man we saw being dragged from the temple! Remember?"

David threw a fig high into the air and watched it fall to the ground. He was thinking of his father and remembering the night in the restaurant when Absalom defended a man by the name of Paul.

"Yes, I remember," David said quietly.

"Tell us what happened to change Paul," Cleon begged Joel.

"Well, he was on his way to Damascus to arrest

Christians," Elizabeth began.

"He honestly thought he was doing right," Mary broke in. "He thought God wanted him to get rid of this little group of Jesus' followers. He went out with hate and murder in his heart."

Joel took up the story, "But, on the road to Damascus with his companions, a great light flashed about him. He fell to the ground. Then a voice from heaven said to him, 'Saul, Saul, why do you persecute me?'

" 'Who are you, Lord?' Saul asked. None of his companions had seen anybody, but they all had heard the voice. The voice continued, 'I am Jesus, whom you are persecuting.' Then the voice told Saul to rise and go into the city, where he would be told what to do.

"Well, when Saul opened his eyes, he was blind; and he had to be led into Damascus. For three days, he couldn't see. He didn't drink nor eat. I guess he must have been doing a lot of thinking. Here he had started out to do one thing, and God had called him to do something else."

Joel stopped for a minute, as if such a wonderful story could not be hurried.

Elizabeth finished it for him. "Then a man named Ananias came to see Saul. Saul's blindness left him, and he received the Holy Spirit. That's about all there is to it. Saul is the man who became the Apostle Paul."

David looked at Cleon and said, “Well, Paul is like any other prisoner now.” David’s fear for his father’s safety was all he could think of. “I’m tired of hearing about him.”

That night, after the evening meal, Cleon, David, and Absalom slept under the stars. The women stayed in the house. All agreed to get up with the sun. The fig picking should be finished before noon.

12

The city of Caesarea was magnificent and colorful. It lay like a great, white jewel against blue sky and water. Its harbor, encircled by great stone blocks, was the main seaport of Palestine.

Herod the Great, who had rebuilt the temple of Jerusalem, had left his bootmark on Caesarea too. Many of the beautiful buildings were brilliant with precious stones and gold and silver. The palace of King Agrippa was there.

There were splendid amusement centers for athletic contests and chariot races. There were enormous and gaudy theaters, where traveling entertainers put on variety shows. It was a gay city, where soldiers and officials could relax.

Cleon looked around him with wide eyes. They passed through the center of town. He could hardly hide his excitement. This was to be his home! In a few more minutes, he would meet the rest of David's family. He was bursting with happiness and curiosity as they walked through the streets.

But there was no conversation between Absalom and David. For the first time since they had left Jerusalem, Absalom rode in one of the carts. He had dismissed the oxen driver at the city gates. David's father did not seem to be aware of anyone but himself. Cleon thought he was probably going over all the things that had happened to him since leaving Caesarea.

Cleon knew what David was probably thinking too. David was worried about his mother. He had refused to talk about the Christians that afternoon on the road. It seemed he was determined not to hear anything more until he knew exactly how his mother felt.

They left the center of town with its long colonnaded shopping street and entered a narrower street, where houses were built in apartment style. Each apartment had a large, separate courtyard.

"Here we are!" David exclaimed. He ran ahead and into one of the buildings.

Absalom's home consisted of two floors. There was a community stable for the carts, horses, and oxen. Absalom got out of the cart, and Cleon walked quietly beside him. His heart beat unsteadily as they tied up the oxen.

David's mother ran out to greet them. Cleon thought she was more beautiful than a goddess. Her eyes and skin were darker than David's. She wore a loose purple garment and white hair covering. Her veil had blown loose, so that every feature was visible. She did not see Cleon as she greeted her husband warmly and hugged her son to her side. They stood in the courtyard, just off the street.

Absalom returned his wife's greeting and, at the same time, drew Cleon into the circle. "We have a new boy, Martha. This is Cleon. He is to be our son."

David's mother took one look at Cleon. Her face paled and her eyes widened. She pulled her veil down hastily to cover her face. "Is not the boy a Gentile, Absalom?" she asked, so low that it was hard to hear the words.

David noticed Cleon squirm uncomfortably.

"Cleon is learning the Scriptures, Mother," David told her. "He wants to become a proselyte."

"Let's go inside," Absalom urged, taking his wife's arm gently. "There is much to tell you. Cleon is only a small part of it."

Martha looked from one to another. Cleon could not see her face now. He smiled at her shyly. "I can be of service to you," he said. "I pray the gods you won't be sorry."

Martha let out a cry and ran into the house. David followed her.

When Cleon realized what he had said, he bowed his head in shame. He had forgotten at the worst possible moment! David had warned him often. He felt ashamed and embarrassed. He had wanted very much to make a good first impression and had hoped David's mother would like him. Now he had ruined it.

"Never mind, Son," Absalom comforted him. "It is easy to slip back into old ways. It won't be long before you'll be one of us. David's mother will grow to love you. I'm sure of it. But we must give her time. When she becomes a Christian, she will not feel as she now feels about Gentiles." He led Cleon into the house and showed him the room he would share with David.

Rebecca, David's sister, was two years younger than David. She tossed her dark hair and tilted her head every time she spoke. "I don't know what I'll do with another brother," she said when they were introduced. "One is too many!" No one told her that Cleon was a Gentile and had been a slave.

Since it was almost the Sabbath evening, Martha was busy in the kitchen. David explained to Cleon that the Jewish Sabbath began at sunset and that no one could work after that time. There must be enough food prepared to last for the next day.

Absalom went to the kitchen with Martha. He talked to her as meat roasted on a spit over an open fire. Cleon could not hear them, but through the doorway, he saw that Martha's veil was thrown back. He could see her lips set in a thin line. She did not appear to answer nor to question. She prepared vegetables and fruits. She set out many kinds of little cakes.

When David and Rebecca went off together, Cleon felt more and more uncomfortable. He did not feel at all the way he had with David and Absalom in Jerusalem, or on the way home. Home! He hoped he would not make another mistake. If only David's mother would give him a chance!

Before they sat down to dinner, Cleon drew away. He knew David's mother did not want him to eat with them. But Absalom insisted. He was the head of the house; so Cleon joined the family. It would be worse to go against Absalom's wishes than Martha's.

Meals at Absalom's house began with hand washing. A large bowl of water was passed around, and each one dipped in his fingers. Then a towel was passed. When they were all finished, David's mother put the bowl and towel away and lit the candles.

Absalom picked up a piece of bread and raised his eyes. "Blessed art thou, O Lord, our God, eternal King, who bringest forth bread from the earth," he said.

Each member of the family said a blessing before drinking the wine.

"Blessed art thou, O Lord, our God, eternal King, who createst the fruit of the vine."

Cleon was miserable. He did not know what to do. He did not know the words. Rebecca watched him as if she could not believe her eyes. Cleon dropped the cup of wine. It spilled to the floor.

After the wine was wiped up, they ate. No one talked during the meal. Cleon could hardly swallow his food. When everyone was finished, Absalom led his family in singing a psalm of thanksgiving. Cleon pretended to sing, but his mouth opened and closed at wrong times. Then Absalom prayed, and the meal was over. The boys were excused.

It was too warm to sleep. David and Cleon went up to the rooftop. They could see the main street of Caesarea. Lanterns lit the tall rows of columns. In the distance, lights twinkled at the harbor.

Cleon spoke first, "I'm sorry about this afternoon."

"It's done now."

"I'm sorry about the wine too. That is a bad omen."

"Will you stop talking like that!" David shouted. "No wonder my mother thinks you're still a pagan. You're always using those heathen expressions."

"I can't help it," Cleon defended himself. "You know I don't really mean them." He remembered Absalom's words: "It's easy to slip back into the old ways." He broke off in sudden panic. What if Absalom slipped back into the old ways? Then Absalom would not have anything more to do with him, either.

"Well," Cleon thought, "I'd better stop feeling sorry for myself. I will make the best of this situation. And I'd better start teaching David some of the things I've promised."

Before they left the rooftop, David explained what would happen in the synagogue the next day. "Someday you'll come with us," he told Cleon, "and you'll hear the rabbi read. We men sit together, but the women are hidden behind a partition."

When they went down to their room, David fell

asleep quickly. Cleon could hear his even breathing and was almost asleep himself when he heard voices in the next room. It was Martha and Absalom. Their voices were low, but Cleon could hear every word they said. He could almost see David's mother, her veil covering her face, timidly facing her husband.

13

"Will it not be humiliating," Martha asked, "a Gentile boy living with us? And now—now this blasphemy about the Messiah?"

"You worry too much about what our friends will say!"

"But will they not think you have turned from the laws of our fathers?" Martha's voice shook.

"Martha, I am still a Jew. I will still attend the synagogue. It just means that the prophecies have been fulfilled. We all find it hard to accept at first because the Messiah did not come in the way we expected. We looked for a mighty warrior to rid us of our enemies."

Martha was silent.

By moving just a little, Cleon could see her through the draperies. He saw her hands fingering her veil nervously.

"I can never hold my head high again," Martha said. Then, "O Absalom, we have always set the example here in Caesarea." She clasped her hands together and leaned forward. Her voice sounded frightened. "Will you force me to turn my back on the Scriptures?"

"I will not force you to do anything," Absalom replied tenderly. Cleon could not see his face, but he heard the great love in Absalom's voice. "I cannot understand why you don't believe me. I was anxious to return home to tell you the good news. Why do you doubt?"

"I don't know." There were tears in Martha's voice. "Perhaps I need time. I don't know enough about it. Perhaps it is the boy—it is all so unexpected—"

"Of course," Absalom said, "it is the boy. It was too great a shock for you. I'm sorry, Martha. But you will come to love him as I do. Please try. In the meantime, I want him to go to the synagogue school with David."

Martha laced and unlaced her fingers. She nodded her head meekly.

Cleon felt better. He leaned back on his mattress. She was going to let him stay. He could hear them talking about other things; then their voices faded. If only there were some way to make David's mother like him. He must try very hard to please her.

The next day was the Sabbath; and, after the family returned from the synagogue, Cleon asked if he could see the city. He even suggested that the family take a walk down to the harbor.

Martha could not hide her horror. Her veil swung over her face. "We do not walk on the Sabbath except to the synagogue," she told him.

The next day, however, the two boys had a chance to explore. David was anxious to show Cleon the sights. The two boys walked down to the docks and watched the great, high-masted merchant vessels which sailed from Egypt and followed the coastline to Rome. There were light, fast warships too, with hundreds of oarsmen.

"It would be fun to be a soldier, wouldn't it?" Cleon asked. In his mind he could see himself in hand-to-hand combat, flourishing a stubby, flat-bladed sword.

"If we were Roman soldiers, we would make all of Parthia bow before us," David said, nodding agreement. "But I'd rather be a soldier in the Messiah's army. Maybe the Messiah will come when I'm grown up. I'd like to see all Rome bow down!"

"But the Messiah has already come," Cleon said. "Your father—"

"That's what you think." David picked up a rock and flung it toward the sea. It disappeared without a splash in the white-capped breakers.

"But you heard your father and Ezra and all those people we met—"

David turned to leave the wharf. "Yes, I heard them, but my mother doesn't believe, and I don't think she ever will," he said.

"But you heard what Ezra said, and Miriam and Ruth," Cleon said. "You can't change what you've heard—or what you believe."

"Then I don't believe!" David said. "Come on. Let's walk up to the barracks. There are soldiers there from all over the empire. We can guess which province from their insignia."

There was little activity around the army post when Cleon and David reached it, and very few soldiers.

"These barracks aren't much better than a stable," Cleon commented.

"Father says the soldiers spend much time at the amusements," David said. "There are many things for them to do in Caesarea."

David led Cleon past the stadiums and theaters. Then they came to the arena. "I saw a chariot race once," David said, "but I've never been to an arena. Have you?"

"Once," Cleon answered. "I didn't like it. I saw a man killed."

"How?" David was wide-eyed.

"They use swords. This man was old and wounded. The people turned up their thumbs. That means the other man can kill him."

"Can the people free them too?"

"If they want to. But they don't very often. Let's not talk about it." Cleon walked on.

Cleon wanted to see the cave David had told him about, where he and his friends had their meetings. Maybe someone would ask him to belong. Maybe they could play soldiers or pirates.

"N-no, not today," David said. "We'll go to the cave some other day."

On the way back to the house, they saw three boys rolling hoops. They were chattering loudly. "There go some of my friends," David said. "They belong to the gang!"

David shouted and ran up to the other boys excitedly. He began to tell them about his adventures in Jerusalem. He seemed to have forgotten about Cleon.

Cleon watched the boys hopefully. He prayed they would like him and talk to him. Cleon touched his short hair. He no longer wore the headdress. He would be glad when his hair looked like theirs.

Finally, David introduced them. The boys looked at him queerly. "Are you a Gentile?" one of them asked.

Cleon nodded his head.

The boy looked at David. "He's living with you?" he asked.

David nodded.

The boys looked at David curiously, then smiled at each other in a secret way. Suddenly, they started to roll their hoops in the other direction.

David did not say anything until they were almost home. Then he turned to Cleon. "Just wait—after your hair has grown out and when you go to school with them, it won't matter that you're a Gentile. They'll ask you to join the gang. If they don't, I'll make them!"

Rebecca was in the courtyard. She had drawn a hopscotch diagram on the hard ground and was playing by herself. When she saw the two boys, she asked them to join her.

David shook his head and went into the house.

Cleon stayed. He selected a pebble for a counter.

He was just about to throw it, when Rebecca shook her dark curls. "What does a pagan temple look like, Cleon?" she asked slyly. "Do you say prayers like ours, or is it true that you throw little children onto the fire?"

Cleon squirmed. He wished David had not left him. He wondered if Rebecca really wanted to know or if she were trying to make him feel like an outsider. He ran his finger across his cheek, feeling the wound that was almost healed.

"I can see where you wore your slave tag," Rebecca taunted. "There's a white ring around your neck." She flung her hair over her shoulder. "You really are different," she sighed. "Come on, Cleon, tell me about a heathen temple."

Cleon's face was red and hot. "A temple . . ." he began, then stopped. "Let's play hopscotch," he begged.

"I've changed my mind," Rebecca said. "I—I don't want to play with you after all. I don't see why you have to live with us and spoil everything!" She brushed past him, holding her head high and lifting her skirts so that she would not touch him.

Cleon sat alone in the courtyard. He pressed his hand to his cheek. Was it his disfigured face? Was it his short hair? What was it that made him different?

He felt just like anyone else. What was the difference between Jew and Gentile? How could anybody really tell—except for his short hair? Jesus did not care what anybody was. Did it matter to God? How could he make Rebecca and the boys see that he loved and hated and hurt the same as anybody else? If he could not, he would have to go away. He could not stand to be forever on the outside, looking in.

14

The next day, David, Rebecca, and their mother went to visit relatives on the other side of the city. David's mother did not ask Cleon to go with them. He knew she did not want him.

When Absalom invited Cleon to walk to the market, he was quick to accept.

"First, I have a letter to give to the brethren here in Caesarea," Absalom said as they walked along the stepping stones on the street.

Cleon knew about the letter but did not say anything. He watched Absalom.

"I want to talk with you, my son," Absalom said.

"I know you are disappointed, and I am sorry. When Martha becomes a Christian—"

"Do you think she will?" Cleon asked eagerly.

"Of course she will," Absalom said. They turned into a wider street which was paved with large slabs of marble. They were near the arena.

"You and David and Rebecca will believe too. I am sure of it."

Cleon wanted to say, "I believe now," but he was afraid. It was really only when he was with Absalom or the other Christians that he believed. When he was alone, he was not sure. There was much he did not understand. Could he become a Christian and not follow all Jesus' commandments? Jesus wanted people to love their enemies. It was easier to hate, and Cleon hated Vitruvius!

"I still don't know enough about the faith to explain it," Absalom went on. "If only I had touched the hem of Jesus' robe—heard Him—even seen Him from a distance. But I was too young. Jesus Christ died over thirty years ago." He stopped and looked at Cleon. "I find it hard to tell you of something that I didn't see and experience. It was only told to me. And yet . . ."

Cleon nodded. He could understand how hard it was to believe something you had not seen with your own eyes nor heard with your own ears. You had to trust the person who was telling you. He thought of Ezra and felt warm inside. Ezra was a man you could trust.

"David has told his mother all kinds of stories. She is afraid for my safety." Absalom put his arm around his new son. "You have heard the stories too, Cleon. The Christians were persecuted; they are still persecuted. Perhaps they always will be. But it hasn't stopped them, Cleon, and persecution never will stop the followers of Christ. When the Spirit leads, marvelous things happen. Persecution has scattered the followers of our Lord, but it has also made many new believers!"

Cleon felt good. Absalom was talking to him as if he were a grown man. They passed directly in front of the arena. Cleon shivered and pressed closer to Absalom. "I know what you mean," he said. "Being a slave is just like being a Christian. It's even worse because you never really belong to anybody. A slave is just a thing."

Absalom took a deep breath and knocked on the door. After several minutes, the door opened cautiously and a woman looked out.

"I have a letter from Jerusalem for the brethren," Absalom said and held it out to her.

She looked at it and then at Absalom. "Is this a trick?" she asked. "Are you not Absalom, the same who mocked us and called us blasphemers?"

"I am Absalom, but I have become a believer," Absalom said quietly. "May I come in?"

The woman invited them both into the house. There were others in the room, three men and three women. They too looked at Absalom with suspicion. But when he told all that had happened, they were amazed.

Cleon watched the happy group and was reminded of the other Christians he had met. These men and women were interested in each other. They were interested in him too. "They love me," he thought, "and yet they have never seen me before!"

After a time had been set for another meeting, Absalom and Cleon left.

On the way home, Absalom stopped at a small shop where he had business to talk over with the shopkeeper. Cleon looked around the store. There were all kinds of beautiful ornaments and perfumes for sale. He wished he could buy something special for David's mother.

Absalom finished his business and watched Cleon. "Would you like to buy something?" he asked.

"Oh, could I?" Cleon pointed to a beautifully carved

shell hairpin. "Your—David's mother might like it."

Absalom laughed. He paid the shopkeeper and handed Cleon the hair ornament. "It is your gift," he said. "You give it to her yourself."

When they reached home, Cleon was glad to see that the rest of the family had returned. He could not wait to give his gift to Martha. She took it gingerly, turning it over in her hands. Then she said, "Only Roman ladies wear such finery."

Tears came to Cleon's eyes. He started to take the gift back, but Martha kept it in her fingers. "Don't cry," she said. "I will keep it. Maybe someday I shall go to Rome."

* * * * * * * * *

Time passed. Hours slipped into days, and days became weeks. Every day, Cleon went to the synagogue school with David. When he was studying, Cleon was happy. He was deeply moved by the passages from the Scriptures he had to memorize. He repeated them with great delight before Absalom, always hoping that Martha would hear him and would also give him credit.

But she never did.

Martha was not unkind to Cleon. She fed him well. She made clothes for him. But she was never the loving mother to him that she was to David and

Rebecca. When they were alone, she seldom spoke. She never smiled. Cleon was sure she would never really like him.

Cleon lost his pale, thin look; but the loneliness in his eyes was replaced by bewilderment. There were many things he was not sure about. At times God seemed as close as Absalom, but David's mother was like Artemis, the pagan goddess to whom he used to pray—cold and distant. What did it all mean? Pagan, Jew, Christian—they were all mixed up.

15

Cleon's hair had grown long and thick. He could walk among the boys now without being looked on as an outsider—a curiosity. But he still had not been asked to join the gang that met in the cave. What was worse, David's old friends now left him out too. David pretended not to care, but Cleon knew he did.

Even Rebecca had stopped taunting him. She tagged along whenever she could. Sometimes Cleon agreed with David that she was a pest.

Cleon and David did not talk about the gang and the cave any more; they looked for other friends. Sometimes they played on the docks or around the public buildings. Here, Cleon was the leader in any game. He had exciting stories to tell too. He quoted from the poets. His very differences had given him a special place.

It was only when they discussed the new religion that the two boys quarreled. Cleon was afraid to say what he honestly thought, for he knew David did not agree. More than anything, he wanted David and Martha to like him.

Cleon noticed that Absalom no longer talked about the new faith to his wife. But Absalom had not forgotten it. He talked to Cleon about it on their many long walks. Absalom retold stories about Jesus and the apostles. He told Cleon that he often shared with other Christians in a service called "the breaking of bread." He no longer seemed fearful or ashamed. Absalom was studying—and waiting.

One day, when they arrived home from school, Cleon found Martha in the kitchen. She had just returned from the marketplace. Her veil was pushed from her face, and she was putting things away noisily. Cleon wanted to show her a torn place in his cloak, but her face was red and angry looking. She did not reply when Cleon greeted her.

David and Rebecca knew something had happened too. They looked at their mother's worried eyes.

When she saw the children staring at her, Martha said, "Your father is the talk of the town! They say he is no longer a merchant but a preacher!" Her voice trembled and she sat down. The three children came close to her. "I thought he had forgotten his experience in Jerusalem. But they say he is stronger than ever. He spends hours talking with his new friends!"

Rebecca said, "Maybe we'll have to beg on the streets for food!" She looked at Cleon.

Absalom entered the kitchen. He had been standing in the doorway.

"My business does not suffer," he said. "It is better than ever. No one will have to beg. I only do what I must!"

They watched him silently.

Rebecca asked, "Is it the guidance of the Spirit, Father?" She sounded important. Rebecca was impressed with the new words she had heard her father and other Christians use.

Absalom sighed. "It is, my child. I have been an honest and a successful merchant for many years. Yet I saw my associates as little more than things." He turned to Cleon. "They were little more than their own merchandise. But now," he looked at his family, "I see them as persons hungry for the truth. I must tell them all I know about Christ Jesus."

Martha pulled her veil down over her face. She did not look at her husband. "The first thing I know," she said to the children, "he'll be preaching on the first day of the week."

"Oh, he has already!" Rebecca piped up. "I followed him last week."

Martha turned away. "It can't be true," she whispered. "It can't be true! You wouldn't turn your back on the religion of your fathers!"

Absalom went to her. "Martha, I was not preaching. I was only telling of my baptism—my conversion. I will continue to attend the synagogue on the Sabbath," he said, "but the Lord's Day too has become a holy day for me now. It commemorates the day Jesus Christ rose from the dead. I must share in the breaking of bread with the brethren."

There was great sadness in his eyes as Absalom lifted the veil from Martha's face. "I wish you would come with me, Martha. Perhaps if you could hear the Word from lips other than mine . . ."

Martha was pale and her mouth trembled. She bowed her head. "I will not have you laughed at, my husband. Please give up all of this. Please forget it," she said.

"Then you will not go?" Absalom asked, and turned away. "Not even once?"

She was silent for a while, then said softly, "I am your wife. It is my duty to bear your shame with you. Yes, Absalom, I will go with you the next time."

So when the time came for the next meeting, Absalom set out, followed by Martha, Rebecca, David, and Cleon.

At least a hundred people were gathered on the banks of a stream a few miles south of Caesarea. It was a happy group of people who had gathered for worship.

Martha's back was stiff with disapproval as she looked around. "It seems more like a pagan festival than the worship of God," she said.

"Our Lord did not ask us to be sad," Absalom replied. "Wait and see how closely the service follows our own. Soon they will read from the Scriptures."

Martha sat down on the sparse brown grass. Rebecca sat close beside her, and the two boys leaned against a tree trunk. Cleon watched David's mother. Her eyes darted back and forth over the scene. Did she disapprove of so many Gentiles?

Prayers were followed by a reading from the Scriptures. They sang a psalm. Then a man got up and told a story. It was about Jesus. He told of the way Jesus taught people to live.

David nudged Cleon when the meeting was all

over. He whispered, "Look! Look! Isn't that the Roman soldier who stopped to talk to us that night on the road, the time they were taking Paul from Jerusalem?"

Cleon followed David's eyes. He nodded. "Yes, it is the same man. So even Roman soldiers are becoming Christians," he said.

David turned away, almost in disgust, and followed his parents.

On the way home, Martha was silent.

Rebecca asked, "Father, if this isn't a new sect, why don't you and your friends meet in the synagogue?"

"Because some of them are Gentile Christians and are not welcome," Absalom said.

"Mother says it's because it's too hard for them to observe our laws and customs," Rebecca said.

Absalom turned to his wife. "You are a good woman, such a devout, godly woman. I can only pray that someday you will know the truth. Only the truth can make you free. We are both unhappy, Martha. It is my greatest wish that you and I will be of one mind again."

Cleon lagged behind the others. He knew that David's mother was unhappy. Had Absalom expected a miracle on her first day of meeting with the Christians?

After that day, Absalom's family went to the gathering of Christians every Sunday. Sometimes traveling evangelists told stories of Jesus of Nazareth, the Son of God. At other times, men came with tales of the work being done by Christians in other cities and even in other countries. Word was spreading far and wide. They told about Peter and Paul and Barnabas, and about Silas and Timothy. Sometimes men like Absalom told the stories of their own conversions.

Martha listened. She huddled inside her cloak, her veil covering her face. Martha listened—but she did not step forward with the other converts.

16

Winter had come to Caesarea. It was becoming cold, now. The Christians stopped meeting out-of-doors and met in each other's homes. But Martha refused to enter any Gentile house.

David's mother made Cleon a new, warm cloak to wear. Even with that, things grew worse in Absalom's family. It seemed to Cleon that there was an open rift, and he was in the middle. Every time he was around, the grownups stopped talking. It must be his fault. It did not occur to him that Absalom and Martha might not want to discuss their differences in front of their children. Cleon was sure he was the cause of it all.

Every afternoon, David found himself taking Cleon closer and closer to the cave to play. It was like a magnet, drawing David near. He liked the boys they played with well enough, but they were nothing like the cave gang. And it was a different group every day. That was no fun. David liked a group that stuck together. The cave gang did, and they never allowed girls around. Now, there was always some boy's sister following them and getting in the way.

One afternoon, as the two friends played a game of tag to keep warm, they found themselves just above the cave. They could hear the boys laughing and shouting beneath them.

"That's the cave," David said. "Sounds as if they're building something."

"I wish they'd ask us to join them," Cleon said.

"They don't mind asking us for help at school, but not here," David complained. "I'd like to help build that fort." He looked down anxiously. The boys were gathering stones and rolling them to the mouth of the cave. They piled them up, to make a defense.

One of the boys looked up and saw David and Cleon. "Hey! Come on down," he called. "Want to help us?"

The two friends looked at each other. They could not believe their ears. The gang was inviting them to join at last! They scrambled down quickly from the ledge.

"We're playing pirates," Asa, the leader, said. "Here, help us roll up the stones. We've got to protect ourselves and our treasure."

The rest of the boys did not seem to mind that David and Cleon joined them. It was just as if they played together every day.

"Now," said Asa when they had finished, "if Cleon is going to be a part of our gang, we'll have to initiate him."

"Yes, yes!" the others agreed.

One of them said, "David hasn't been here for a long time. We have a new password."

"We'll initiate them together," said another boy. They looked at Asa.

Asa stepped up. "We're playing real pirates this time," he said. "If you want to belong to our gang, you have to get something that belongs to somebody else."

Asa held up his hand for silence. Everyone was quiet. "We need a lantern," he told Cleon and David. "You can find one in a courtyard somewhere. Don't come back without it!"

Cleon and David nodded and ran off. They were so excited about the initiation that they could not think of anything else. The gang wanted them! They would be able to play in the cave every day!

Before they had gone very far, David stopped and kicked at a pebble.

"What's wrong?" Cleon asked.

"I don't want to belong that much, I guess. It—it's really stealing," David said.

"Maybe we could get a lantern from your house," Cleon suggested hopefully. He too stopped walking.

"Maybe we could, but—but it's still stealing," David said slowly.

"It's a part of the game." Cleon was disappointed. "It's the only way we can belong." He brightened. "We can return the lantern later."

David was not listening. "And I thought they really wanted us. I'll bet not one of the others would steal a lantern. That's why they used us. That Asa! He probably planned it this way."

Cleon finally understood. "You're right, David. It would be stealing. I wouldn't want to belong now. Let's go back and tell them."

They turned around and walked slowly back toward the cave.

"Where's the lantern?" Asa asked.

"We're not going to get one. It's stealing," David answered.

"They don't want to join us, boys!" Asa announced. "What'll we do?"

"Hm-m, my father says they're Christians," one of the bigger boys said. "Let's get rid of them!" He picked up a stone and flung it.

Soon all the boys in the gang were throwing stones. One hit David just below the eye. There was nothing for Cleon and David to do but run.

When they reached safety, David said, "I hate them. Sometimes I hate my father too for getting us into this mess. We'll never be safe, now."

"Unless we show them we don't care," Cleon said.

"Or get even with them." David started to pick up a stone. "Come on. Let's stone them!"

The two boys worked quickly to gather ammunition. They filled their tunics with stones of all sizes and started back to the cave. The boys were still playing below.

David reached into his tunic and drew out a jagged rock. He drew back to aim. But at that moment, Cleon grabbed David's arm. The stone fell to the ground.

"What's wrong with you?" David almost shouted. "I thought you wanted to get even."

"I don't want to any more," Cleon said. "I've been thinking and remembering. Jesus said to love our enemies." He let the stones fall from his tunic. "I don't really hate them."

David looked at his friend in astonishment. "Then you are a Christian," he said slowly. He let his own rocks drop to the ground.

"I don't know," Cleon answered thoughtfully. "You can't be a Christian unless you are baptized and belong to the church—but I guess I want to be."

The two friends turned and started for home. With no warning, David's sister was suddenly dancing about on the path before them. "I saw you! I saw you! They threw rocks at you, but you were too frightened to fight back."

"We were not afraid," David said. "You just don't know anything. And besides, why do you always have to tag after us? Now don't go tattling to Mother."

"I won't." Rebecca stood still and looked at her brother. "She'll see your eye, though, and you'll have to tell her what happened. O David, it's all black and blue."

David told his mother the whole story. When Absalom came home, Martha scolded him. "Even the children must suffer because of you," she said. Her voice was clear and strong. She showed him David's eye. Then she told him the reason David and Cleon had not thrown stones back at the boys.

She seemed pleased with them.

Absalom laughed. "You are becoming a Christian in spite of yourself, Martha! Already you express yourself much as a Christian woman!"

The way he said it made Martha laugh too, and the boys and Rebecca joined in.

"It's true," David whispered to Cleon later. "Mother never used to say a word about anything. She left all the talking to Father. Nothing is the same any more. I wish Father had never gone to Jerusalem. If Mother does become a Christian, then she'll be in danger too." David looked away.

17

That evening a knock sounded at the door. Absalom answered it and returned with a stranger. It was one of the men Cleon had seen at the house of the Christians.

"I have come to warn you, Brother Absalom," he began. "It may soon be unsafe for you and your family here."

Absalom motioned to the man to sit down while Martha and the children stood by in startled silence.

"Since the Apostle Paul has been here, some of our own members are rebellious. They feel that the charges against him are unjust. . . ."

"There are no honest charges against him!" Absalom said with feeling. "The Governor Felix allows Paul's friends to attend his needs. Felix himself sends for Paul often to discuss the Way."

"Perhaps he hopes that Paul will give him money in exchange for freedom," the other suggested.

Absalom laughed. "That will never happen! Not if Paul has to appeal to Rome!"

"Nevertheless," the man continued, "our views are not too popular. If you continue to work—"

"I will not run away," Absalom stated. "I am not a coward."

"No one doubts that, Brother Absalom. Paul himself was lowered over the Damascus wall once to escape his enemies. Several time during his journeys, he was forced to flee. It is no disgrace to hold one's life dear."

Martha picked up her needlework to keep her fingers from shaking.

"You can appreciate your husband," the man addressed her. "He is becoming one of the most useful men we have. Paul is no longer young, and he is under arrest. His yoke must fall on others if we are to carry out our Lord's commandments."

"You are suggesting that I go abroad to tell of the Gospel?" Absalom's eyes were bright.

"Yes, you and your family," the other returned. "Of course, we will see what the brethren at the church in Jerusalem would say."

"I—I must think about it," Absalom said quickly. "I must pray and receive the Spirit's guidance."

The stranger stood up and walked toward the door. "There are many people in distant cities waiting for someone to bring them the Word of our Lord and Savior," he said. "We will talk about this mission again. In the meantime—be careful!"

As soon as the stranger had gone, Rebecca said, "Are we really going to leave Caesarea, Father, and all our friends?"

Martha bit the thread from her needle. "Do you expect us to follow you around like—like tentmakers?" she asked. She no longer seemed to be afraid to speak freely with her husband. "Surely, God does not expect so much from you!"

"But, Mother," Rebecca said excitedly, "Father is in danger here! The man said so."

"How do you know for sure what the Lord wants you to do?" Martha asked Absalom.

Absalom bowed his head. "I do not know," he said. "I must depend on the Spirit to lead me, and if it is the will of God that I go, His grace will strengthen me for this difficult task.

"Everyone is given the Spirit for the common good," Absalom continued. "One may be given wisdom to speak or to teach. Another may be given the power to heal. Just as the body has many members, so are we members of the body of Christ. Each of us, with his own gift, is as important as another. I do not know what I must do. I must wait."

Martha and Rebecca set out the evening meal. They went through the prayers and the songs as usual, but everyone was deep in his own thoughts.

After dinner, Martha and Rebecca were busy in the kitchen. Cleon felt awkward and out of place. He went to his room to study.

Absalom turned to the light to examine the bruise beneath David's eye. "It could have been worse," Absalom said to his son. "The skin isn't scratched."

"I wish I'd have hit one of them!" David muttered.

"Would that have solved anything?" Absalom asked.

"I suppose not," David said reluctantly. "But it would have made me feel better."

Absalom was quiet as he looked at his son. It had been a long time since they had talked together, he thought.

Suddenly David burst out, "I don't see how you can take everything so calmly. This man says your life is in danger. I just don't understand why you don't fight back or—or run away or something."

"When I fight, I will use new weapons. I will wear God's armor. If I ran away, I would only be running away from myself," Absalom said. "Can you understand that?"

"No. I can't understand. I can't understand why you are ready to risk your life for a man who wouldn't even fight for his own life—"

"David, David," Absalom interrupted. "Jesus is the Christ!" He paused. "I know you are trying to understand. I know you are fearful too. You are afraid our family may break up in disagreement as some already have done. But there is no reason to be troubled or afraid, David." Absalom put his arm around his son's shoulder. "Loving Jesus and following Him does not necessarily mean being carefree and living an easy life. What it does mean is that no matter how great the danger or how heavy the burden, He will give us strength to bear it. That is what I have learned through my new faith.

"To some faith comes early. To some late. To some—perhaps not at all. I do not know. I will never try to force you nor your mother nor Rebecca to become Christians. But I believe you will someday."

David raised his head and looked into his father's

eyes. "Thank you, Father," he said. "I do not share your faith, and perhaps I never will. I know now, though, that you are searching for the truth and that you will never ask me to believe what is against my conscience."

Martha sent the children to bed early that evening, but David and Cleon could hear the adults talking long into the night. They disagreed; they agreed. They even laughed together at times. But nothing was settled.

Martha had the last word. "Nothing has been the same since you returned from Jerusalem with that boy," she said. "Everything is changed now."

After the house was silent, Cleon lay still for a long time. It was all his fault, he thought. No wonder Martha disliked him. This home was a happy one before he came into it. Even David had said nothing was the same any more. Cleon had been a constant reminder to Absalom. If he were out of the way, Absalom might return to his old life. David's family would be out of danger. There was only one thing do—and that was to leave.

The next day after school, Cleon went down to the docks. He had to be alone to think. Where would he go if he went away? What would he do? The sun disappeared behind threatening clouds. The winds were chill. Cleon huddled inside his cloak, watching the war galleys. Perhaps he could be an oarsman.

He could always lose himself in Caesarea. It was a large enough city. He might look for work near the foothills. He thought about the house where he and Absalom had delivered the letter. That was on the outskirts of the city. The Christians liked him. They seemed to want him. Surely they would help him. They considered themselves one big family.

Cleon stopped. No, he would not go to the Christians. It was the Christians' fault that all of this happened. "If there had been no Jesus Christ, there would be no problem," he thought.

Across the city, the temple of Artemis loomed high against the hills. Maybe he ought to offer a sacrifice to Artemis or another one of his gods or goddesses. Maybe life was too complicated for one God to handle. He dug at his cheek in defiance. At that moment, he hated everything and everybody!

Should he tell David he was leaving? David had been good to him. He and David were like brothers. He wished he had not met David. It was David's fault too that he was here. If David had not helped him to begin with—No, he would not tell his friends he was leaving. It would only cause him pain.

At that moment, Cleon saw a two-masted sailing

vessel in the harbor. The wind tugged at the sails, making them roll and curl like great, white leaves. He thought he had never seen anything so beautiful.

He started toward the pier to get a better look at it. Two sailors walked past him. Their voices carried on the wind.

"This is no time to ship out," grumbled one. "I'd like to stay for the winter."

"Nobody's forcing you to go," the other sailor replied, "but you're as anxious as the rest of the crew to help the captain set a new record."

"We'll be lucky to make it to Myra before winter sets in."

The second sailor looked up at the sky. "The captain is determined to make it to Puteoli, winter or not. Don't forget, the merchant pays an extra bonus if his cargo is delivered to Rome this season."

Cleon considered. Would it be possible to stow away in the hold with the cargo?

Suddenly, he heard a familiar voice. He had not heard it for months, but it brought back memories as vivid as though they had happened yesterday. It was a loud, nasty, bellowing voice.

Cleon turned around. Not two yards away from him stood his master, Vitruvius!

18

Cleon darted down the long pier from Vitruvius. He must get back to Absalom immediately. He ran, thinking of nothing but his own safety. Had Vitruvius seen him? Had he recognized him? Cleon put his hand to his cheek. The scar! Vitruvius might have seen it and remembered. Cleon was panting and out of breath, but he did not stop until he reached Absalom's home.

Once inside, he looked around wildly. There was no one about. Was Vitruvius following him? Cleon's throat hurt. He could hardly swallow. Where was Absalom? He ran through the house, calling his name. Finally, he remembered. Absalom was seldom at home at that time. Where was David? At least David should be there.

But the house was silent. Maybe something had already happened to Absalom and his family, Cleon thought. Then, in a sudden burst of terror and loneliness, he sat down and tried to keep from crying.

In a few minutes, he felt a cool hand on his aching head. Cleon looked up, frightened. It was David's mother.

Cleon jumped up in surprise and stared at her. He saw that her eyes were warm with understanding. He thought he must be dreaming. She put her arms around him. Cleon felt that he should pull away, but he could not. He put his head on her shoulder and wept.

"What is it, Cleon?" she asked tenderly. "What is it, my son?"

"I just saw Vitruvius, my master," he told her between sobs, "at the docks."

"But you are our boy now," she comforted. "We won't let harm come to you."

Cleon stopped crying and looked up at her. "B-but I thought you didn't like me," he said. Tears still ran down his cheeks.

Martha wiped them away. "I was afraid," she said,

"afraid of what my friends would say, afraid that God would condemn me. I was wrong."

Her fingers traced the scar on his cheek. "In the short time you have been with us, I have learned to love you like my own. God works in strange ways. He can transform our lives through love. Perhaps if you had not come to me in trouble, I would not have known yet how much I do love you."

Cleon wiped his eyes. He had never known until this minute exactly what he had missed. It was good to be loved. It was wonderful to have a mother.

He thought about Absalom. Absalom would be happy at this change in Martha. "Are you going to become a Christian?" he asked her.

"I don't know," she answered.

The next few hours were the happiest Cleon had ever known. He stayed close beside Martha, helping her with small tasks around the house. Not once did they mention Vitruvius. Both knew a decision would be up to Absalom. He would know what to do.

Instead, they talked and planned for the future. Martha told Cleon that she would not stay behind. She would go wherever her husband went. If he wanted to continue the work of the apostles by helping to establish new churches, she was ready to go. If he wanted to stay in Caesarea, she would stay with him.

It made Cleon feel good to hear her talk. The way Martha put it, no matter where they went, they still would be in the same family. The people might have different faces, but they were all a part of God's family.

When Absalom, David, and Rebecca came home, Martha told them what had happened. "Must you do anything at all?" Martha asked her husband. "If we are to leave soon, Vitruvius won't know that Cleon is in Caesarea."

David and Rebecca sided with their mother.

"Cleon will have to stick close to home until we leave," David said.

"We'll have to hide him, and we won't let anyone know where he is," Rebecca added.

Absalom had not said a word. David and Rebecca looked at him.

Finally, Absalom spoke. "That would not be according to God's way. Cleon still belongs legally to his master."

"But can't you buy him from Vitruvius?" pleaded Martha. "Cleon is like our own son, now." She put an arm around him.

Absalom looked at them. He saw tears in Martha's eyes. He saw her shining face.

Martha nodded. "Yes, Absalom," she said. "I am

ready to listen now. I want you to tell me more about your new belief."

"Thank God," Absalom said softly.

"We shall see Vitruvius in the morning," he continued after a moment. "If God be with us, who can be against us?"

Everyone agreed with Absalom, and all slept soundly that night.

The next morning, as Absalom and Cleon prepared to leave, Martha touched her husband's arm. "Go quickly, my husband, and bring Cleon back safely to his home," she said.

"Yes, Martha," he answered. "I am praying God will let that happen."

* * * * * * * * *

At first, it seemed as if they would never find Vitruvius. Cleon knew Absalom was right to look for his master, but he hoped they would never find him. They searched the docks; they went to the public buildings. Cleon prayed that he had made a mistake, that it really was not Vitruvius he had seen. But after several more inquiries, they found Cleon's Roman master at the army depot. Absalom and Cleon waited in an outer room while a soldier went to get Vitruvius.

Vitruvius was as fat as ever. Even his toga could not hide his roundness. His small, beady eyes narrowed when he saw Cleon. Then he scowled. When he looked over at Absalom, Vitruvius' face changed. He tried to smile, but it was an effort.

"I looked for you in Jerusalem," Absalom began, "but you had gone. I would like—"

Cleon tried not to tremble as he faced his master, but his knees were weak.

"Thank you for taking care of the boy so well," Vitruvius said. His voice was oily. "I did leave suddenly. There was not time to search for him. Poor thing! He must have been frightened when he found me gone."

Absalom tried to speak, but Vitruvius cut him short. "I sent him on an errand, and he got lost. I disliked leaving without him. He is one of my best scribes."

"I wish to buy him from you," Absalom stated flatly.

Vitruvius appeared to be thinking. He stroked his chin with one hand. He looked at Cleon. There was hate in his eyes.

Cleon's heart beat faster.

"He is worth a great deal to me," Vitruvius said. "I have one of the largest libraries in the empire. This slave's work is good. I need him."

19

"I'll pay you anything," Absalom said quietly.

Vitruvius tried to smile again, but his eyes remained beady. "It might be arranged," he said. "Five thousand denarii?"

Absalom looked startled. Cleon drew a deep breath. That was a great deal of money! Did Absalom have that much? Would he think Cleon was worth that amount? He watched Absalom with fear in his eyes.

"I did not bring that much with me," Absalom said. "I shall return with the money immediately."

"Tomorrow morning will be soon enough,"

Vitruvius said. "I must question my slave about one of the manuscripts he was working on. If you will excuse us—," he dismissed Absalom and reached for Cleon.

Absalom took Cleon's arm. "I will be back tomorrow with the money, Son," he said. "God be with you."

Cleon went with Vitruvius. He knew his master was going to flog him. Cleon shivered. Maybe he would be dead by the time Absalom returned. Maybe he would never see Absalom again.

Inside a smaller room in the barracks, Vitruvius locked and bolted the door. He turned to Cleon, his face red with anger. His round stomach shook with fury. "So!" he screamed. "You return of your own free will, thinking that in this way I will release you! Bah!" He grabbed Cleon's shoulders.

"You disguised yourself with long hair and Jewish customs so that I would not know you. Why did you return?"

"My master is God," Cleon said miserably. "To obey Him, I must obey you."

"Well, I hope all escaped slaves take over this strange belief and come back to me. Because of you, I lost two more slaves. By the gods, I hope they become Jews and return also! I'll show them!" he repeated, his face red with anger. "Nobody makes a fool of Vitruvius!"

He hit Cleon again and again until the boy fell to the floor. "Pray to your new God now!" He laughed wildly. "Ask Him to save you!" He gasped for breath. "Today we leave for Rome!"

Then it was all just a trick! Cleon was sure of it now! Vitruvius planned to be gone when Absalom returned with the money!

Vitruvius kicked the boy and left the room. Cleon heard the big bolt slide in place. This time, there was no escape.

How long he lay there, Cleon did not know. He was dazed with pain. He knew Vitruvius would not kill him. He would get more enjoyment out of making him suffer. And the manuscripts! Soon he would be copying until his fingers ached. He would never dare make a mistake again.

Cleon tried to remember a Psalm, but there was no comfort in it. He tried to pray, but the words stuck in his throat. God had been cruel to him. Jesus had come to earth to tell people how much God loved them. Was this love?

There were noises outside the door. Cleon cringed. How could he go through more punishment? The door opened. Vitruvius pushed another slave toward Cleon. It was an older man. It was Alexander, the shopkeeper in Jerusalem!

Vitruvius bound them together. "You two won't get very far if you decide to run away," he laughed. Then he left.

"Cleon, is it really you?" the older man asked.

"Alexander! How did Vitruvius get you? Was it my fault? Did he discover that I was in your shop?"

"No," Alexander answered, "he won me from my master in a dice game. I belong to Vitruvius now." He laughed bitterly. "In the flash of a few minutes, my whole life changed. I pray the gods that each night will be my last."

Cleon looked at his friend and felt sorry for him. Cleon hated Vitruvius now more than he had ever thought possible. He was sick with hatred. It boiled in his stomach.

Alexander continued, "My former master was kind to me. I was buying my freedom. He tried to buy me back, but Vitruvius only laughed in his face. All Romans are not like Vitruvius. When we reach Rome, perhaps we will be able to escape."

"Is it true that other slaves ran away?"

"Yes, two have escaped. But that does not anger Vitruvius so much as that he is being returned to Rome because of his temper. He cannot get along with the officials, either. He leaves Palestine in disgrace."

Cleon sighed. "I guess that means he'll make it

harder than ever for us," he said.

Soon Vitruvius came for them. He walked Cleon and Alexander, still bound together, through the streets of Caesarea toward the docks. People stared but not for long. They were used to such sights. For a brief moment, Cleon wished that Absalom or someone he knew would be in the crowd. No one would ever know what had happened to him.

Cleon and Alexander were led up on the pier. They were put into a small boat and rowed out to a large merchant ship. It was the same one Cleon had watched only yesterday. It rose high above the water at both stem and stern. There were two cabins on the top deck—one for the captain, the other for important passengers.

Vitruvius was outranked and had to stand on deck. It was crowded with men who could withstand the discomfort for as long as it took to sail to Rome. Cleon and Alexander, still bound, were crowded into the middle of the deck. The hold was full of cargo and prisoners with their guards.

"Hoist the sails," ordered the captain. "Weigh anchor!"

The sailors followed his orders, and they were under way.

Cleon watched the proceedings dully. Before, when

he had sailed, it was exciting. He had enjoyed the gently rippled sea give way to mountains of foaming spray. He had loved the sound of the wind singing in the rigging. Today, it was different.

The wind pushed them along the coast, and Caesarea faded away into nothing. The sturdy vessel dipped her bow majestically between the ridges of the waves. Salty spray glistened in their hair, and the taste of it was on their lips. Sea gulls circled over the ship, then flew toward shore.

"You haven't told me yet how you got to Caesarea," Alexander said to Cleon. "Tell me—what has happened to you?"

Cleon was slow to answer. But Alexander asked question after question until Cleon was forced to tell the older man the whole story from his escape to the present. He told him about Absalom and the new belief.

"This Messiah you speak of must have quite a few followers," Alexander said. "I have heard of His teachings. Some of our philosophers in Athens have the same ideas."

A man who had been standing next to them, turned around to face Alexander. "Bah!" he said. "Some say we are nothing but puppets. The stars or the moon or the sun guides each of our lives."

Cleon looked at the man in astonishment. He wondered how many others had heard his simple story of Christianity. He was thankful Vitruvius was not near. "Are you a Christian?" Cleon asked the stranger.

"No," the man answered, "I have never heard of this Man you call the Christ. But . . . ?" He leaned closer and whispered, "I like what I have just heard."

Alexander turned around toward Cleon and asked, "Is a Christian free to think and act as he pleases?"

Cleon hesitated. "Yes, he is. I never thought about it before. A Christian is always free—even if he is a slave. Vitruvius does not own my soul," he added.

"Perhaps you can tell us more, my boy?" Alexander invited. "All of us would like to hear what you have learned."

Cleon sighed. Caesarea was disappearing in the distance. So were his hopes. "I can't tell you very much. You see, I'm not quite convinced myself," he said. "Nothing has worked out the way I planned it, Alexander. It really doesn't matter, one way or another."

20

The next morning, Vitruvius untied the ropes that bound the two slaves together. "We're safe enough out here," he laughed, looking out over the blue sea. "Just try to escape!"

Alexander shuddered. Cleon said nothing. He had dreamed the night before of getting even with Vitruvius. But he could not remember how he had done it. How could one man, a Roman master, be so hateful? Cleon asked himself. Was he to spend the rest of his life looking for revenge?

The merchant ship sailed on slowly. Vitruvius paid

no attention to Cleon and Alexander except to give them food. He was on his best behavior. Both slaves knew why. Vitruvius had become acquainted with the officials who had the cabin, and Vitruvius wanted a space there.

The coastline of Asia Minor was dimly visible. Cleon wanted to cry out with misery and hopelessness, but Alexander asked for more stories of his adventures. Jason, the man who had overheard them the night before, sat nearby on the deck. He told them he was on his way to Rome. Jason too asked questions. It helped to pass the time.

Cleon was surprised that he was able to remember so many stories about Jesus. Each one reminded him of another that some traveling evangelist had told. Cleon could remember almost every one. As he retold stories, it made the Man Jesus more real to Cleon. Jesus was a Person, not a figurehead. He was a Man who had lived and suffered and died. Jesus had many enemies, but He did not waste time trying to figure out ways to get even with them. He loved them. He prayed for them. And He tried to teach His followers how to get along with themselves and with their neighbors. As all of it came alive to Cleon, he wondered if the teaching of Jesus Christ would spread throughout the whole world. "Who knows?"

Cleon thought. "It might."

Toward sunset, Vitruvius came upon them suddenly. The vessel rolled heavily in a ground swell, and he lost his footing. He fell on Cleon. Vitruvius picked himself up awkwardly. His face was red, and he looked embarrassed. But his embarrassment soon turned to anger.

"You!" he said to Cleon. "I hear you're telling stories about your new God. Well! Tell me about Him too. I'm your master. Tell me about Him."

The crowd pressed in closer. Vitruvius preened himself. His voice grew louder. "Tell us about your new God!"

The captain came up. He sneered at Vitruvius. "We can use the services of all the gods on this trip," he said. He looked at Cleon. "What specialty has this God of yours?"

"Yes, tell us, tell us. Tell us about your God," the passengers cried.

Cleon bit his lip. His hands shook. What could he say? Everyone was looking at him. Vitruvius looked as though he were going to pull the words from Cleon's lips.

"God loved the world so much that He sent His Son, Jesus Christ, to earth—," he began.

"Jesus? The Christ? That's the Messiah the Jews

are looking for." It was a voice in the crowd.

"Go on!" commanded Vitruvius.

"Well, Jesus taught God's way, but very few people believed that He was the Messiah. They put Him to death. On the third day, He rose from the dead. People saw Him. He returned to His Father, but He sent the gift of the Holy Spirit to those who believed in Him. He gave them the strength necessary to carry out His work. Anybody who believes shall receive the Holy Spirit. It's like having Jesus right beside you to guide you." Cleon stopped.

"The slave has become a rabbi!" Vitruvius laughed.

"What must we do to be saved?" someone mocked.

Cleon bit his lip harder. "You must repent of your sins and be baptized," he said in a loud, clear voice. "You must join the company of believers. . . ." He could not finish.

Jason smiled a little. "I don't understand all of that. You'll have to do a little more explaining to convince us," he said.

While Cleon had been speaking, the rolling of the ship had grown worse; now it pitched violently. The wind stopped singing, and howled. The waves crashed over the bow, drenching the decks and the passengers. The captain shouted orders. The sailors scrambled to their stations.

"It's only a squall," someone said. "No need for alarm."

But it was more than a squall. A wild wind struck from land. Before the sails could be lowered, the mainmast had snapped like a twig. The tangle of lines and canvas was cleared away; but, even so, the wind caught their freeboard and carried the ship dizzily before it without direction, without control. Everyone listened to the fearful sound of straining timbers.

It grew dark. The rain came down in torrents as the ship faced mountain after mountain of black, swirling water. Lightning flashed. Deafening thunder and the sound of the gale cut short any further conversation.

The men huddled together in fear. They cried out to the gods to save them. They shook with terror, and still the storm raged. The ship pitched and rolled. Every minute seemed to be the last, but the endless night continued.

Suddenly, there was a lull in the storm. "Lighten the ship!" ordered the captain. "Throw out the cargo!"

The precious cargo was thrown overboard. All eyes watched. All men gasped in disbelief.

Then, as suddenly as it had started, the storm was over.

A thick, heavy quiet lay upon everyone. A dense fog covered them. The mainmast was broken; the sails a mass of torn wreckage. They were helplessly adrift.

Day stretched into night and the night was reaching for day again. There was no sun; there were no stars. Someone had found an oil lamp and a tinder set. The faces of the men who sat around the light were tired and frightened. They did not look at one another; they only stared at the small lamp.

"Where are we?" bellowed Vitruvius, as if his anger could demand an answer.

"I don't know," answered the captain wearily. "We've tried to cast out the anchor, but it's too deep."

"We'll never get out of this alive!" one of the passengers cried.

"We may hit a reef in this blackness," said another.

Panic spread. "Would that we had perished in the storm!" someone cried. "We'll starve to death now."

Vitruvius stumbled over the huddled men until he reached Cleon. "You!" he shouted, kicking him. "You're bad luck to all of us—you and your new God! I command you to return to the worship of your old gods! Pray, slave, pray, before we all perish!"

Someone threw an image of the goddess Artemis at Cleon's feet. He picked it up and turned it over in his hands. It was a pretty trinket with a single, bright jewel; but that was all.

21

Suddenly, someone shouted, “Land!” All eyes searched the water. Day was beginning to break. A light breeze had come up, and the fog was lifting. They could tell east from west. Sure enough, a faint shadow of land was there to the left of them.

The passengers shouted with joy. Men hugged each other. “Land!” they cried, tears running down their faces. “Land!”

Cleon did not join the excitement. He was praying. For the first time, he was able to remember a prayer. It was the prayer Jesus had taught His followers: “Our Father which art in heaven. . . .”

Everyone strained for a glimpse of shore. No one spoke.

"Hoist the jury sail!" the captain ordered. "Ease the rudder lines." Then he ordered a sounding taken. Twenty fathoms (about 120 feet)! Then fifteen fathoms. The bottom was shoaling.

At that minute, the big ship struck a sand bank. The men fell forward with the impact. The bow stuck, shuddered violently, and the ship was fast. The surf began to break up the stern. Men shouted and screamed and clung to the rail, not knowing what to do. This was the worst moment of all.

"All of you who can swim, throw yourselves overboard," commanded the captain. "Make fast for land! Those who can't swim will have to use planks from the ship."

There was a mad scramble as men toppled over the side of the vessel. Some of them tore loose planks from the ship. Others stood, panic stricken, afraid to move.

"Hurry! We're sinking fast," the captain shouted.

Already black rats scurried up from the hold.

"Can you swim?" Cleon asked Alexander.

The older man nodded.

"We'll meet on shore," Cleon said. "God be with you." He dived into the cold water.

The sea was full of bobbing heads. Men kicked, floated, and swam. They had to be careful to keep out of the way of the rough planks.

Suddenly, Cleon heard a bellowing voice behind him. It came from the ship. He turned around. It was Vitruvius. Standing alone on the tilting deck.

"I can't swim," he yelled. "Somebody help me!" The ship was sinking fast. The water reached Vitruvius' ankles.

Cleon paddled, dog fashion, as he watched the man he hated. His chance to get even with Vitruvius had come. There was no one around to help him. Even the captain was halfway to shore.

Cleon saw the ship tremble and crack. It was breaking apart. "Help me!" cried Vitruvius. His voice was weaker. Water was up to his knees now.

Cleon knew he could save Vitruvius if he wanted. He could swim back and tow his master to shore. Water made a man light. Cleon could manage. It was the kind of thing Jesus would do. Jesus said to do good to those who treat you badly. Jesus would probably save Vitruvius.

Cleon turned and started for shore again. "Save Vitruvius for what?" he asked himself. "So that, for the rest of his life, Vitruvius can bully his slaves? Vitruvius is mean! He does not deserve to live,"

Cleon thought. If Vitruvius did not reach shore, then Cleon, and Alexander too, would be free. Cleon could then go back to Absalom's family. Alexander could go to Athens. It was his duty now to think of Alexander. Alexander was no happier with Vitruvius than Cleon was.

If Vitruvius asked him for help, he would help him. He might not want to, but he would. But this was different. Vitruvius could not see him. Vitruvius was calling anybody. Cleon could say he thought his master was safe on shore. It was not his business. Had not the captain said every man for himself?

"Help!" Vitruvius sounded weaker.

Cleon looked around and saw that water was up to Vitruvius' waist. Before Cleon knew what he was doing, he found himself swimming toward the ship as fast as he could go. " 'Thou shalt love thy neighbour as thyself.' " Whether he liked it or not, he and Vitruvius were brothers.

"Jump!" Cleon called up to Vitruvius. "I'll help you."

Vitruvius was too frightened to look surprised. He leaned over awkwardly and fell headfirst into the water. When he came up, he was sputtering and fighting. "What are you trying to do, slave, drown me?"

Cleon found it difficult to tow Vitruvius because he

struggled and his toga was heavy with water. Cleon wished he had a plank. It would be easier.

"Cleon! Is that you?" It was Alexander, swimming toward them. "I missed you. I was afraid you were in trouble." Then Alexander saw Vitruvius. He swallowed a mouthful of water in his surprise.

Vitruvius kicked and sputtered. "Stop struggling," Alexander said as he swam beside him. "We'll get you to shore safely. Don't worry!"

With that, Alexander brought up his fist and punched it into Vitruvius' fat jaw. Cleon and Alexander paddled along with Vitruvius between them. "Sometimes you have to hit a man, master or slave, when he fights you," Alexander said, spitting out a mouthful of water. "This time it gave me great pleasure."

Cleon could not see Alexander, but he knew the older man was grinning.

They touched bottom. Cleon and Alexander dragged Vitruvius between them up onto the beach.

When Vitruvius regained consciousness, he sputtered. He shook his head, and water spurted from his nostrils.

Cleon watched his master closely. He felt strangely light and free. Cleon no longer hated Vitruvius! Instead, he felt sorry for him.

Cleon looked away and out to sea. He saw the ship settle down into the water. Vitruvius looked up and saw it too. He shuddered. For once, Vitruvius was without words.

Someone had built a fire farther on up the beach. Cleon and Alexander, with Vitruvius between them, worked their way up to it. The passengers who had survived the shipwreck were warming themselves. They were close to a village, for people kept appearing with dry clothes and words of comfort. Cleon heard one of them say they were Christians.

"Where are we?" Vitruvius finally asked.

One of the villagers answered, "Dora—just up the coast from Caesarea."

"Back where we started!" Vitruvius said. "It seems impossible!" His voice was beginning to get back some of its harshness again.

Vitruvius walked over to Cleon. "Why did you do it, slave?" he asked.

"It is as I told you," Cleon answered directly. "I have two masters now—God and you."

"I don't understand that kind of talk," Vitruvius said uncomfortably and waved his flabby arms, "but I do understand that I owe my life to you—and Alexander." He turned to Alexander. "You two are no longer slaves. You are free. Now leave! Get out of my sight!"

Vitruvius walked away quickly.

Somehow it was not a surprise to Cleon and Alexander that they were free.

Cleon said with a smile, "Where are you going, Alexander?"

"To Athens." Alexander smiled back. "As a freedman. Will you come with me?"

"No," Cleon answered, "I'm going home."

"Home?" Alexander asked. "You mean to Absalom?"

"Yes," Cleon answered. "But I have another home now—among the company of believers in our Lord and Savior Jesus Christ."

Cleon started down the road which led to Caesarea. He had been gone only a little over three days. He was sure Absalom and David and Martha and Rebecca would be waiting for him. If not, he could find them through the Christians. Christ's family would soon be all over the world.

Cleon knew he would never be lonely again. He knew now that no one need ever be lonely.